A BIBLIOGRAPHY

OF

HORACE WALPOLE

BY

A. T. HAZEN

and
DAWSONS OF PALL MALL
Folkestone, England
1973

First Published 1948
Reprinted by permission of Yale University Press 1973

Dawsons of Pall Mall
Cannon House
Folkestone, Kent, England

Distributed in the U.S.A. 1973 by
Harper & Row Publishers, Inc.
Barnes & Noble Import Division

ISBN: 06 492760 1

copyright, 1948 by Yale University Press

Printed in Great Britain
by Photolithography
Unwin Brothers Limited
Old Woking, Surrey

PREFACE

QUITE *early in editing the Yale edition of Horace Walpole's correspondence, we saw that a full-dress bibliography of Walpole's writings and the productions of his private press was badly needed. This project, which Mr. Hazen undertook for us in 1939, is completed with the present volume. The* Bibliography of the Strawberry Hill Press, 1942, *and the* Bibliography of Walpole *should be considered ancillary to the larger work.*

Although it is true, as Mr. Hazen points out in his Introduction, that this second volume lacks some of the spectacular aspects of the first, Mr. Hazen has made extensive additions to the Walpolian canon and thrown added light on Walpole's earlier writings. My final review of this second volume was made—owing to a temporary loss of eyesight—by the aid of my wife who read the entire work aloud to me. Bibliographies are not often regarded as suitable works for reading aloud, but even though I do not pretend to be an adept in the mysteries and excitements of collations, I found this account absorbing. It is readable, I think, not only because Mr. Hazen's style and method are so easy to follow, but because it is a biography as well as a bibliography. One forgets that Horace Walpole was a man of letters as well as a letter-writer, but the reader of the present work is not likely to overlook it in the future.

This volume reveals no forgeries and little of the biblio-

graphical hanky-panky which enlivened its predecessor, but it is not without its surprises and drama. How many of its readers, one wonders, had expected to find in it the most popular poem in the language, Gray's Elegy? *Louis XVI translating* Historic Doubts on Richard III *in the Tuileries not long before his death is a picture familiar to Walpolians, but the story of young Dominique Corticchiato completing in Paris, at the age of seventeen, his translation of the* Castle of Otranto *before being taken up and destroyed by the Germans will be new to them. Mr. Hazen, who is a member of the Advisory Committee of the Yale Edition of Horace Walpole's Correspondence, has placed Walpolian studies on a secure foundation and he has shown again how valuable a tool bibliography can be.*

W. S. LEWIS

Farmington, October 1947.

CONTENTS

Introduction	7
Books by Walpole	17
Books with editorial contributions by Walpole	103
Contributions to Periodicals, &c.	153
Books dedicated to Walpole	169
Apocrypha	171
Unprinted manuscripts	175
Index	179

ADDENDA AND CORRIGENDA

Page 31. The *Norfolk Tour* was published in four earlier editions, in 1772, 1773, 1777, and 1786.

Page 61. What seems to be the sixth copy on vellum of the Bodoni edition, bound in tree calf, has just been ordered by WSL from an English bookseller.

Page 136 should read as follows:

55. LETTERS OF EDWARD VI. 1772.

HW wrote the 'Advertisement.' For description see the *SH Bibliography*, p. 99.

56. MISCELLANEOUS ANTIQUITIES. 1772.

HW wrote the 'Advertisement' in No. 1 and the Life of Wyatt in No. 2. For description see the *SH Bibliography*, p. 103. In the British Museum (Add. MS 12528) is an account book showing receipts and disbursements of the Duke of Buckingham during his various embassies, 1622–28. HW has inscribed it: 'I bought this MS of Mr. Thoresby's nephew, 1764'; and on the cover: 'Curious Papers collected for my Miscellaneous Antiquities.' But he did not print this material; the MS was sold in 1842, SH Sale, vi. 125.

INTRODUCTION

I. The bibliography of Horace Walpole and the bibliography of the Strawberry Hill Press.—II. The variety and importance of Walpole's writings.—III. Arrangement and method.—IV. Additions to the Strawberry Hill Bibliography.—V. Abbreviations.—VI. Acknowledgments.

I

IT is impossible to think of a bibliography of the writings of Horace Walpole apart from the work of his private press at Strawberry Hill, since so many of his own books were printed there, or, to reverse the point of view, since so many of the books printed at the Press were written or edited by Walpole. I therefore planned to study both groups of books, and when I began to work in 1939, a principal decision to be made was whether to study the Strawberry Hill Press books first and then make references to that bibliography when I turned to the study of Walpole, or whether to begin with Walpole's bibliography and then make references to that. The Strawberry Hill bibliography came first, largely because in 1939 the status of the thick-paper copies of Gray's *Odes* was in doubt, and an attempt to solve that bibliographical puzzle was immediately challenging to a bibliographer's pride.

The *Bibliography of the Strawberry Hill Press* was published in 1942, plentifully sprinkled with unresolved doubts on bibliographical points, but at least representing a careful attempt to develop a consistent theory of bibliographical investigation from the minutiae of a limited problem. In 1942 I expressed the hope that the next part of my work would be a bibliography of Horace Walpole's writings; and it is now a satisfaction to be able to fulfill that promise.

Since cross-references had to be made, whichever part of the work was published first, it is pointless to apologize for the number of items that are included here merely as references to the *Strawberry Hill Bibliography*. I regret that this volume cannot be used without frequent reference to the other; but it was never any part of our plan to repeat detailed collations in the second book. Since this book has to depend in certain ways on the earlier one, it has seemed proper to maintain the same arrangement and format so far as possible. It is partly for this reason that I seem to have given no consideration to two suggestions of reviewers about arrangement, though perhaps personal preference helps to make the uniformity of the two volumes seem more important to me than a small improvement.

As they now stand, the two books together form in effect a two-volume Walpolian bibliography.

II

MUCH of Horace Walpole's writing was ephemeral, and much that was important was so closely bound up with the confused politics of the time that it retains little interest now for the average reader. It is worth observing, too, that his books sometimes stirred more interest than their intrinsic worth warranted: the *Castle of Otranto,* despite its tinselled gloss, is historically important because of its influence. Or, in a smaller way, his pretended Letter from the King of Prussia to Rousseau, which was written only as a joke among friends, became the immediate cause of the unedifying quarrel between Hume and Rousseau, two of Europe's leading philosophers.

But Walpole's work is of major importance to all who are in any way concerned with the political, social, or artistic history of the eighteenth century. His historical *Memoirs,* left in manuscript for posthumous publication, comprise perhaps the most valuable single commentary on English politics from 1750 to 1790; they are written from the Whig point of view but without rancorous Whig prejudice, an honest and careful account by an observer and participant who was watching the

INTRODUCTION

causes of men's actions. His *Correspondence* preserves our fullest record of the social life of the time, full of gossip and triviality but full also of acute comments on men and women, on books and authors, on antiquarian studies and contemporary events.* His *Catalogue of Royal and Noble Authors* and his *Anecdotes of Painting* rescued from the wasteful dissipation of time a great mass of important biographical detail. And it is to Walpole's editorial and typographic zeal that we owe the *Life of Lord Herbert of Cherbury,* as well as most of the poems of Thomas Gray. In this volume, therefore, are the bibliographical records of diverse books both lasting and ephemeral, the records of a man who never lost his interest in political changes and new cultural phenomena, in antiquarian research and in the imaginative power of fiction, in society gossip and occasional verse. There are in fact a good many verses here, especially in the list of unprinted manuscripts at the end, that will necessarily be included in any new edition of *Horace Walpole's Fugitive Verses.*

Partly from their topical nature, Walpole's books have not had any wide and continued appeal, and the political pamphlets have never been eagerly sought by collectors. Of the books included in this volume as being written or edited by Walpole, only the two by Gray and the *Castle of Otranto* are today widely sought by general collectors. In this bibliography, therefore, the provenance of copies will not be so fascinating as it was in the *Strawberry Hill Bibliography:* the most eagerly sought item recorded here is of course Gray's *Elegy,* but unfortunately no copy seems to have any important contemporary association. Somewhat related to this matter is the fact that certain books seem unreasonably common because they are sought by collectors and scholars: the Parmesan *Castle of Otranto* of 1791 is listed in every volume of *Book Prices Current,* although only three hundred copies were printed; but the edition, probably larger, printed at London in 1791 is unknown to *Book Prices Current* and is not easily found today.

* It is of some interest that Walpole, the chief of letter-writers, was asked by Dodsley to furnish a preface to Chesterfield's *Letters;* but he declined. See his letter to Mason, 27 November 1773.

[9]

BIBLIOGRAPHY OF HORACE WALPOLE
III

FROM the bibliographical point of view this volume will seem less interesting than the Strawberry Hill volume. Here are no late reprints to be sold as originals and no outright forgeries. Perhaps only two items included here, *Aedes Walpolianae* and Bentley's *Designs for Gray's Poems,* can be called particularly interesting bibliographically. Very few cancels are described, and almost no variant issues. The interest in this volume, I believe, will be found instead in the history of Walpole's literary career, a man well aware of political and historical problems however much he emphasized mere gossip and occasional verse.

It is unfortunate that such widely scattered and diverse matter cannot be made to appear logically consistent in a descriptive bibliography. Only a chronological arrangement has any value in portraying an author's literary growth, since no logical division by types is practicable in a bibliography. On the other hand, an occasional poem or epitaph, published in a London newspaper years after it was composed, has little significance if it is crowded between two books published at that time—and the user of the bibliography is merely confused, no matter whether he is searching for one entry or studying Walpole's career. Somewhat regretfully, therefore, I have planned the volume in three main sections: 'Books by Walpole,' 'Books with editorial contributions by Walpole,' and 'Periodicals.' Such a division, partly by physical appearance or manner of publication, is I hope not unduly confusing, and it offers some conveniences. Contributions to the *World* are entered under 'Periodicals,' even though Walpole had some slight editorial interest in that paper; in other words, physical appearance has been given precedence over logical classification, so that the reader can find in the third division any item not issued as a single, separate publication. I have extended the category 'Periodicals' to include poems in anthologies. In the Index I have prepared an analytical grouping by indexing numerous kinds of publication; in the Index this will not interfere with the large chronological series in the text.

Short poems and other occasional squibs that appear only in editions of the *Correspondence* or in Mr. Lewis's edition of *Walpole's Fugitive*

INTRODUCTION

Verses (1931) have been omitted; they are separately recorded only when they were first printed elsewhere. In other words, this is a bibliography of the separate printings of Walpole's writings, not a table of contents of his *Correspondence*. At the end of the volume I have placed a brief list of Walpole's unpublished manuscripts, but it may be a proper precaution to point out here as well that unpublished short poems and fragments not included in that list exist in various collections.

The facsimiles of the title-pages (of the first two divisions) are again planned to obviate the need for long transcriptions, and the printed titles are therefore kept as brief as may be. The spelling has been normalized in quotations from the letters and from Walpole's 'Short Notes.' Measurements, although they are not very important, have been recorded whenever an untrimmed copy has been available.

The facsimiles are the same size as the originals whenever possible; when a reduced facsimile has been required, the amount of reduction can be discovered by comparing the width of the facsimile with the measurement of the widest line of the original as recorded below the facsimile. Most of the facsimiles have been made from copies at Farmington. The rest have been made, with the kind permission of the owners, from other copies, as follows: No. 3 (Harvard); No. 17, the first state of Bodoni's title-page (Huntington Library); Nos. 12 and 63 (New York Public Library); No. 8 (University of Illinois); Nos. 1, 15, and 58 (Yale); and No. 41 (the C. B. Tinker–Yale copy). No facsimiles have been prepared for books printed in the twentieth century.

The method of bibliographical description is the same as that used in the *Strawberry Hill Bibliography:* the total is always the same in the collations by signatures and by pagination, but the semicolons do not necessarily match in the two collations. A bracketed signature means that no leaf of that gathering is signed.

IV

As opportunity offers, some corrections or additions to the *Strawberry Hill Bibliography* are inserted in this volume. Such notes will not make this a second edition of the *Strawberry Hill Bibliography* or render the earlier volume obsolete. The earlier volume as it stands is substantially correct if (as I earnestly hope) I have found more errors in it than anyone else; but it has seemed that there might be some interest in a few additions that can be logically fitted into this volume.

No references are included in this volume to the Detached Pieces printed at Strawberry Hill. Any user of the two volumes will be aware that many of the Detached Pieces were Walpole's own compositions, but to insert all the references in the chronological sequence would have cluttered this volume badly, at very slight gain in our understanding of Walpole's career. Their omission is therefore justified on practical if not on logical grounds. I have records of some additional copies of certain Detached Pieces, but no evidence to suggest any significant change in their relative scarcity: four labels and cards of which I had seen no copies in 1942, Nos. 66, 73, 76, and 77, are in a collection in the Boston Public Library.

Walpole's own collection of Detached Pieces has now been found just where it ought to be, in the library of the late Lord Crewe. I have seen the collection only in a copy on microfilm, but the typography can be examined on film. My compressed summary in this paragraph may serve as a supplement to the *Strawberry Hill Bibliography*. Walpole's collection includes most of the first forty items in my numbered list of Detached Pieces; nearly all the rest of the Detached Pieces were prepared by Kirgate on his own initiative. Walpole's collection contains no copies of Nos. 20, 23, 24, 26, 29, 31, 32, 34, 35, 38; some of these are not under suspicion, but the absence of Nos. 24, 26, 32, 34, and 35 strengthens the doubts I cast on those five pieces in 1942. My doubts about the authenticity of Nos. 1, 5, and 14 are confirmed now that I find a different setting of type in Walpole's collection. Walpole's copies of Nos. 2, 3, 7, 11, 13, 21, 27, and 33 are of course original. No. 9, 'Painting in Oil,' which I suspected to be an earlier, rejected form of No. 10, is marked by Walpole, 'This was not used.' No. 16, the Epitaph on Lord Waldegrave, is an entirely different setting; the copy illustrated in the *Strawberry Hill Bibliography* may therefore be a Kirgate reprint. No. 18, containing the verses by Pentycross, is at the very end of Walpole's collection, and so my conjecture that this was a

INTRODUCTION

much later printing than 1768 is confirmed. In addition to No. 25, the ticket to view the house, there is a copy of another form that was not used. Nos. 39 and 40 are at the end, save for No. 18, and both have notes in Kirgate's hand; they are therefore confirmed as late printings initiated by Kirgate.

The most important correction to be made at present in the description of the Detached Pieces is in No. 87, the title-page for *Etchings by Lady Louisa Augusta Greville;* Walpole's copy of the volume, untraced since 1851, reappeared late in 1942 and is now at Farmington. The title-pages (three besides that for Lady Louisa's etchings) were printed at Strawberry Hill; possibly the copy of the one title-page in Lord Waldegrave's collection was reprinted by Kirgate. Now that we know how the book looks, it becomes possible to match it with HW's letter to Mason, 7 May 1775: 'I have just made a new book. . . . It is a volume of etchings by noble authors. They are bound in robes of crimson and gold; the titles are printed at my own press, and the pasting is by my own hand.' The identification is thus completed, and the book can be dated.

Some new evidence about the nineteenth-century forgeries (*Strawberry Hill Bibliography*, pp. 151–8) of ten Detached Pieces, which I dated between 1818 and 1880 and probably before 1840, suggests that they were all prepared *ca.* 1818.

V

For convenience in frequent reference, I have made use of the following abbreviations:

HW.=Horace Walpole.
HW's Fugitive Verses.=*Horace Walpole's Fugitive Verses,* collected and edited by W. S. Lewis, Oxford University Press, 1931.
Lowndes.=*The Bibliographer's Manual of English Literature,* by W. T. Lowndes, revised by H. G. Bohn, 1857–64.
SH.=Strawberry Hill.
SH Bibliography.=*A Bibliography of the Strawberry Hill Press,* by A. T. Hazen, Yale University Press, 1942.
SH Sale.=*Catalogue of the Classic Contents of Strawberry Hill,* 25 April to 21 May 1842 (sold by George Robins). The roman and arabic numerals indicate the day and lot number. (A parenthetical 'London Sale' refers to the

prints and illustrated books of the Seventh and Eighth Days' Sale, withdrawn and recatalogued for sale in London, 13–23 June 1842.)

'Short Notes.'—Horace Walpole, 'Short Notes of the Life of Horace Walpole.' This MS was first printed by Richard Bentley in the fourth volume of the *Letters to Mann,* Concluding Series, 1844; the original MS, differing importantly from the printed text, is now at Farmington, and will shortly be published in the Yale edition of HW's *Correspondence with Gray.* My quotations are from this new recension.

Waldegrave MS.—In Lord Waldegrave's collection there are thirty folio volumes of Walpolian MSS; they include his historical *Memoirs,* largely published, and six volumes of transcripts of Walpole's letters to Sir Horace Mann. I have examined only three volumes, brought to Farmington by Mr. Lewis in 1943, but these three are undoubtedly the most important for my purpose. The first is a commonplace book begun in Italy in 1740; the second, entitled *Poems and other Pieces by Horace Walpole,* contains Walpole's transcripts with notes of most of his occasional pieces from 1736 to 1756, a record that was started about 1742; the third is a similar volume of transcripts of his political papers during the same period. Since all my references are to the second or third of these three volumes, and since the nature of the text differentiates the two, I have indicated only that a piece is transcribed in the *Waldegrave MS.*

Waller Collection.—Items recorded as having been in the Waller Collection can be identified more fully in the sale catalogue, Sotheby's, 1921. Pieces referred to in the text as having been in the Waller Collection, with no further identification, were bought in by the owner in 1921; they were resold at Christie's, 15 December 1947 (after this book was all in proof), and are now at Farmington.

WSL.—W. S. Lewis, or in the collection of W. S. Lewis at Farmington.

VI

IT is pleasant to record here that my bibliographical work has been made easier by courteous and friendly help wherever I have turned. Civilian travel has been so restricted that I have completed this work on the basis of the evidence so richly spread before me in Farmington, corroborated by what I could find in New England, New York, and Chicago. I am glad to bring together the records of my indebtedness to the various libraries, records that are scattered through the pages that follow: to Harvard, Yale, Columbia, the Metropolitan Museum of Art, the Morgan Library, the New York Public Library, the Newberry Library, the University of Chicago, and the University of Illinois. Particularly at Yale and the University of Chicago have the

INTRODUCTION

members of the staffs helped me and gladly forgiven me my odd bibliographical inquiries. I owe a particular debt for answers to specific inquiries about books in their care to the following: Mr. H. R. Archer of the William Andrews Clark Memorial Library; Mr. Roland Baughman, formerly of the Huntington Library and now of Columbia; Mr. Curt Bühler of the Morgan Library; Mr. P. B. Daghlian, formerly of the University of Rochester and now of the University of Indiana; Mr. Frederic Goff of the Library of Congress; Mr. H. Guppy of the John Rylands Library; Mr. Karl Küp of the Spencer Collection in the New York Public Library; Miss Alice S. Johnson of the University of Illinois; Miss Lucy E. Osborne of the Chapin Library at Williams; Mr. Arthur Wheen of the Victoria and Albert Museum; Mr. Ralph Williams, formerly of Wellesley and now of Trinity College in Hartford; and Mrs. Gertrude L. Woodward of the Newberry Library. Many other friends have responded from time to time when I have needed help, all of whom I would thank for their advice and encouragement: Mr. C. H. Bennett, Miss Emily H. Hall, Mr. Nicholas L. Heer, Mr. George L. Lam, Mr. C. P. Rollins, Mr. W. H. Smith, Mr. C. B. Tinker, Mr. A. Dayle Wallace, and Mr. W. K. Wimsatt, all of Yale; Mr. T. W. Hanson of Pulborough, Sussex; Mr. J. P. Kirby, formerly of Mary Washington College and now of Randolph-Macon; Mr. R. W. Chapman of Oxford; Mr. G. D. Hobson of Sotheby's; Mr. A. N. L. Munby, formerly of Sotheby's and now Librarian of King's College, Cambridge; and Mr. A. J. Watson of the British Museum. Many notes in this book are based on Mr. W. S. Lewis's examination of books in England, and he has besides advised with me constantly and read the manuscript; it is a pleasure to acknowledge all his help, as well as the continuing hospitality he and Mrs. Lewis have offered in their home and library. Miss Julia McCarthy has helped unfailingly in my work in the library at Farmington, and my wife has worked over every page of my text with me. The bibliographical judgments expressed in the book are my own, but every page is cooperative in terms of the people who have helped me.

A. T. H.

The University of Chicago,
  June, 1947.

*BOOKS
BY WALPOLE*

THE
LESSONS
FOR THE
DAY.

BENG THE

First and Second Chapters of the Book of
PREFERMENT.

LONDON:

Printed for W. WEBB near St. *Paul*'s. 1742.
[Price Sixpence.]

1. REDUCED. WIDTH OF ORIGINAL 11.8 cm.

BOOKS BY WALPOLE

1. THE LESSONS FOR THE DAY. 1742.

'Short Notes': 14 July [1742]. I wrote *The Lesson for the Day*, in a letter to Mr. Mann; and Mr. Coke [Edward Coke, M.P., 1719–1753], son of Lord Lovel, coming in while I was writing it, took a copy, and dispersed it till it got into print, but with many additions, and was the origin of a great number of things of that sort.'

The *Lesson* (HW wrote only a single chapter or lesson, although two were printed) was a satire on William Pulteney and his friends as place-hunters. Pulteney, after years of parliamentary struggling against Sir Robert Walpole, was maneuvered into the House of Lords, 13 July 1742, as Earl of Bath. He was immediately attacked in numerous pamphlets and ballads, and lost his political influence. HW's use of Biblical parody was possibly suggested by *The Chronicle of the Kings of England,* by Nathan Ben Saddi, 1740–41, probably written by Robert Dodsley.

In a note added later to his letter to Mann, 14 July 1742, HW wrote: 'This piece, with a very few additions, was the original of a numberless quantity of the same kind, which were published upon all subjects for a year or two.' In a note to his own transcript of his satire, in *Waldegrave MS,* HW wrote: 'This piece was wrote by Mr. Walpole in a letter to Mr. Mann . . . the morning of these promotions, which were the second made after Sir Robert Walpole's resignation. A copy got about, and was printed in two chapters with great additions, by whom he does not know; but this was the original of those swarms of papers in the same way, that came out on all subjects for a long time afterwards.'

HW to Mann, 28 August 1742: 'The *Lesson for the Day* that I sent you, I gave to Mr. Coke . . . and by his dispersing it, it has got into print, with an additional one, which I cannot say I am proud should go under my name.' In the printed text, of two lessons or chapters, the second is largely HW's.

Besides the MS sent to Mann in the letter and HW's somewhat revised transcript in *Waldegrave MS,* there was a copy of the revised text in HW's hand, in the Waller Collection; Dr. Toynbee printed this in 1918 in his *Supplement to the Letters of HW,* ii.78.

Folio; published 5 August 1742, for sixpence; approximately 31.5 x 19.7 cm. untrimmed.
Signatures: [A]–C².
Pagination: [1] title-page; [2] blank; 3–12 text.

 I think that this well-printed folio, so unlike the carelessly printed editions described below, was the first edition, perhaps sponsored by whoever added the first chapter. It may have been sent to the printer by Sir Charles Hanbury Williams, in whose collected *Works* the text was reprinted. I have examined copies at Harvard and Yale, and there is a copy at Farmington. Not only is this edition better printed than the others and so according to general bibliographical probability likely to be the first edition, but it matches the announcement in the *Gentleman's Magazine* for August of a pamphlet published by Webb at sixpence. Webb might have published a very shabby little octavo pamphlet for twopence or threepence and then been shamed into reprinting it as a fine folio, I suppose, but it seems unlikely. Other editions have an extra line on the title-page, 'Read to a Congregation at St. James's,' a phrase likely to have been added, not removed. Ordinarily the second of the editions described below would be accepted as the first because HW owned it, but he is so explicit in denying any knowledge of the printing that he seems fully as likely not to have had a copy of the first edition.

OTHER EDITIONS

 1. Octavo, 12p.; one half-sheet unsigned and a quarter-sheet signed B. The title-page follows the first edition down to the imprint, which reads: 'Printed in the Year MDCCXLII.' Like the other editions in octavo, it is badly printed.

 2. A copy pasted into HW's *Waldegrave MS*. This edition is on cheap paper, one half-sheet, octavo, with horizontal chain-lines. It is badly printed, with glaring misprints, wrong-fount letters, and broken type. The title-page adds: 'Read to a Congregation at St. James's.' The imprint reads: 'London: Printed for W. Webb near St. Paul's. 1742,' without any price.

 3. A copy very similar to HW's, printed from the same setting of type but with two errors corrected, is in the New York Public Library.

 4. At Farmington there is another edition, one half-sheet, octavo.

The imprint reads merely: 'Printed in the Year, 1742.' This is an entirely different edition: it has mistakes enough of its own, but they are not the mistakes of the previous edition, to which it is probably unrelated.

5. The copy in the British Museum is one half-sheet, octavo, with horizontal chain-lines; but the title-page reads like No. 1 above. At Haigh Hall there is (or was) an edition of seven pages in folio, printed for Webb; this would seem to be an imperfect copy or a compressed reprint of the first edition.

6. The text was reprinted in the first number of *The Foundling Hospital for Wit*, 1743, and in the *Works of Sir C. H. Williams*, 1822, iii.28.

7. It seems likely that an edition was also published in the Low Countries with a new title, to judge by the following letter from H. S. Conway to HW, dated from Ghent, 15 September 1742: 'I have seen your chapter of preferments printed here, and the additional one, which is not bad neither—a pompous edition and a new title, *The Vision.*' (The Conway letters were printed in *Fraser's Magazine* for June 1850.)

CONTINUATIONS

HW wrote Mann, 28 August 1742: 'Nothing but *lessons* are the fashion: first and second *lessons,* morning and evening *lessons,* epistles, etc.' The first and second lessons, of course, were the two *Lessons* described above; HW's text is incorporated in the second. I list here such continuations or parodies as I have records of:

The Evening Lessons for the Day, being the Third and Fourth Chapters of the Book of Preferment. By the Author of the First and Second. Webb, 1742. A variant title reads merely *The Lessons for the Day* . . . but has the same text. The copies I have seen are bound (and no doubt were issued) with the New York Public Library and WSL editions of the original pamphlet. There may also be a folio edition, since the *Gentleman's Magazine* for August 1742 lists *The Evening Lessons,* published by Webb for sixpence.

The Lessons for the Day, being the Fifth and Sixth Chapters of the Book of Preferment. By the Author of the foregoing. Webb, n.d. Bound (and necessarily issued) with the New York Public Library's edition of the original pamphlet.

BIBLIOGRAPHY OF HORACE WALPOLE

The Evening Lessons, being the First and Second Chapters of the Book of Entertainments. A satire on Vauxhall and Ranelagh, published by Webb for sixpence, 11 August 1742, and reprinted in the *Foundling Hospital for Wit,* 1743.

Lessons for Evening Service, 1742. This sixteen-page pamphlet in the British Museum is still another satire written as a Biblical parody.

The Epistle for the Day, being part of the Second Chapter of the Acts of the Patriots. Another satire on Pulteney, in the *Foundling Hospital for Wit,* 1743.

A Lesson for the Day, being the Second Chapter of the last book of the Chronicles of the Kings of France and England. By Michael Ben Haddi, 1744. The title must have been suggested in part by HW's squib and in part by Dodsley's *Chronicle of the Kings of England.*

[H. Fielding?] *A New Lesson for Pope.* Sent to Mann by HW, 28 August 1742 as 'a very good one' on Cibber's letter to Pope.

2. THE BEAUTIES. 1746.

'Short Notes': 'In July . . . [1746] I wrote *The Beauties,* which was handed about till it got into print, very incorrectly.' According to Daniel Wray, HW's authorship was generally known; see his letter quoted in J. Nichols, *Illustrations,* i.100.

Although the lines were addressed to the painter, Eckardt, they seem to have been composed particularly for Lady Caroline Fox. HW sent the verses to her in a letter to her husband, Henry Fox, 19 July 1746. Fox and Lady Caroline welcomed them enthusiastically, and Fox wrote HW immediately that he planned to make them public. On 24 July HW replied to Fox, begging him on no account to make public such hastily composed trivia; he did not want to incur the enmity of all other ladies, he protested, and the final lines on Miss Elizabeth Evelyn were too particular. He ended his letter to Fox: 'I am, my dear Sir, and always shall be, if you will suppress my verses, your most obliged humble servant.'

HW's note to his transcript, in *Waldegrave MS,* reads: 'Wrote in July 1746. . . . Some copies of this poem having got about, it was printed without the author's knowledge, and with several errors. It was reprinted more correctly in the second volume of a Miscellany of poems in three volumes published by Dodsley 1748.' The folio edition, despite a few small errors, is in general very close to this MS copy. Another MS copy, in an unidentified hand, was sold at Hodgson's, 24 August 1944.

HW to Mann, 12 November 1746: 'Don't scold me for not sending you those lines to Eckardt; I never wrote anything that I esteemed less, or that was seen so incorrect; nor can I at all account for their having been so much liked, es-

THE
BEAUTIES.
AN
EPISTLE
TO
Mr. *Eckardt*, the Painter.

LONDON:
Printed for M. COOPER, in *Paternoster Row.* 1746.
[Price Six-pence.]

Enter'd in the Hall-Book of the Company of STATIONERS.

2. REDUCED. WIDTH OF ORIGINAL 11.9 cm.

pecially as the thoughts were so old and common. I was hurt at their getting into print.'

But if HW was at first hurt by seeing his verses in print, he bore up extremely well; he included them both in his *Fugitive Pieces*, 1758, and in his *Works*.

Folio with horizontal chain-lines; published by M. Cooper at the beginning of September, at sixpence; an untrimmed copy measures approximately 37.4 x 24.5 cm.
Signatures: One leaf unsigned; B²; one leaf unsigned. The title-page and last leaf were probably printed together.
Pagination: [1] title-page; [2] blank; 3–8 text.

EDITIONS

Dodsley printed a somewhat corrected version in his *Collection of Poems*, 1748. HW also reprinted the poem in his own *Fugitive Pieces*, 1758, and in his *Works*, 1770 and 1798; it was included in the third volume of Bell's *Fugitive Poetry*, 1792; and in *HW's Fugitive Verses*, 1931.

COPIES

The copy at Farmington is untrimmed, so that one can be certain the poem was printed on half-sheets of a double-size paper. Another copy, at the University of Michigan, has been cut down severely.

3. EPILOGUE TO TAMERLANE. 1746.

'Short Notes': 'November 4th and 5th [1746], Mrs. Pritchard spoke my Epilogue to [Rowe's] *Tamerlane* on the suppression of the Rebellion, at the theatre in Covent Garden; it was printed by Dodsley the next day.'

HW's note in *Waldegrave MS:* 'Wrote at Windsor. . . . *Tamerlane* is always acted with an occasional prologue in honour of King William, on the 4th and 5th of November, being the anniversaries of his birth and landing. This epilogue was spoken on those two days in honour of William Duke of Cumberland, who had defeated the Young Pretender in Scotland in the foregoing April. It was printed the next day by Dodsley, and afterwards by him in the second volume of his *Collection of Poems.*'

HW to Montagu, 3 November 1746: 'Just now I am under the maidenhead-palpitation of an author; my epilogue will, I believe, be spoke to-morrow night, and I flatter myself I shall have no faults to answer for but what are in it, for I have kept secret whose it is. It is now gone to be licensed, but as the Lord Chamberlain is mentioned, though rather to his honour, it is possible it may be refused, as they are apt to think at the office, that the Duke of Grafton can't be mentioned but in ridicule.'

EPILOGUE
TO
TAMERLANE,
ON
The Suppression of the Rebellion.

SPOKEN
By Mrs. *PRITCHARD,*

In the Character of the Comic Muse, *Nov.* 4. 1746.

LONDON:
Printed for R. Dodsley at Tully's-head in Pall-mall; and sold by M. Cooper at the Globe in Pater-noster-Row.

[Price Sixpence.]

3. REDUCED. WIDTH OF ORIGINAL 14.3 CM.

HW to Mann, 12 November 1746: 'I enclose you an epilogue that I have written. . . . *Tamerlane* is always acted on King William's birthday, with an occasional prologue; this was the epilogue to it, and succeeded to flatter me.'

Foolscap folio; published 5 November, sixpence.
Two sheets unsigned.
Pagination: [1] title-page; [2] blank; [3]–7 text; [8] blank.

Editions

HW's Epilogue was reprinted in the fourth number of the *Foundling Hospital for Wit*, 1747; in the second volume of Dodsley's *Collection of Poems*, 1748; in HW's *Fugitive Pieces*, 1758; in the *Works*, 1770 and 1798; and in *HW's Fugitive Verses*, 1931.

Copies

The copy at Harvard, which I have collated, has been trimmed by the binder, but it is a good copy; it was bequeathed to Harvard by E. J. Wendell. There is also a copy in the British Museum. I have found no trace of HW's copy; possibly he preserved only his MS copy in *Waldegrave MS*.

4. AEDES WALPOLIANAE. 1747.

HW compiled a list of pictures at Houghton, with their dimensions and the artists' names, in 1736; this MS is now in the Morgan Library, inlaid in HW's copy of *Aedes Walpolianae* 1752. By 1743 there were additional pictures, and HW appears to have reëxamined the whole collection. He was at Houghton through most of the summer of 1743, and the dedication of the volume to his father is dated 24 August 1743. (Sir Robert died in March 1745, before the volume was printed.)

Perhaps to add interest to his volume, HW then added a short piece he had written in 1742. See 'Short Notes': 'In the summer of 1742 I wrote *A Sermon on Painting*, for the amusement of my father. . . . Afterwards published in the *Aedes Walpolianae*.'

HW's note to the *Sermon on Painting* in *Waldegrave MS*: 'This sermon was preached at Houghton before Lord Orford, and is a sort of essay on his collection of pictures there. 1742. It has since been printed in the *Aedes Walpolianae* 1747. The second edition of which was published 10 March 1752.' [The last two sentences were added later.] There are a few very small variants in the text of this MS. Another MS of the *Sermon* is with HW's letters to Montagu, at Kimbolton.

Next, HW decided to include in the volume John Whaley's poem, *A Journey to Houghton;* see Whaley's letter to HW, 12 September 1743: 'I have a copy of the verses at Kingsland. . . . I will endeavour to make them as much better as

ÆDES WALPOLIANÆ:

OR, A

DESCRIPTION

OF THE

Collection of Pictures

AT

Houghton-Hall in *Norfolk*,

The SEAT of the Right Honourable

Sir *ROBERT WALPOLE*,

EARL of ORFORD.

---

*Artists and Plans reliev'd my solemn Hours;
I founded Palaces, and planted Bow'rs.*
                    PRIOR's *Solomon.*

LONDON: Printed in the Year 1747.

4. REDUCED. WIDTH OF ORIGINAL 14.1 cm.

I can, and dress them up as clean as possible that they may appear with decent modesty, in company so far above them as you will condescend to introduce them to.... I purpose leaving out the trifling circumstances of the journey and leave nothing in the poem but what relates to Houghton if you think proper, which I should be glad to know.'

'Short Notes': 'In 1747 I printed my account of the collection of pictures at Houghton, under the title of *Aedes Walpolianae*. It had been drawn up in the year 1743. I printed but 200 copies, to give away. It was very incorrectly printed; another edition, more accurate, and enlarged, was published 10 March 1752.'

Although the numeral is very distinct in the MS of 'Short Notes,' so that the number '200' is unmistakable, I think HW in writing years afterwards made an error. His list of recipients in his own copy, now in the Dyce Collection, has eighty-three names, and his note at the top is written out distinctly: 'There were but one hundred copies printed.' Furthermore, he wrote to Mann in August 1748: 'I have just printed an hundred'; and Vertue's bill (now wsl) for the engravings specifies 100 copies of each.

DATE

The date on the title-page is 1747, but the printing was delayed by corrections which necessitated cancels. Furthermore, the plates are dated 1748, and Vertue was not paid for them until November 1748. In the list of recipients (in HW's copy, now in the Dyce Collection) 85 of the hundred copies printed are listed, and HW kept at least two or three. He did not send Mann's copy (sixteenth in the list) until October 1748; and the other three for which we have the date of presentation (Sir Danvers Osborn, William Cole, Prince of Wales—all 1749) are well down in the list. So it seems unlikely that any copies were finished in 1747, despite the date on the title-page. From the collation one can surmise that Signature A containing the title-page was printed first, not after the text had been completed. No doubt the book was printed (begun, at least) in 1747, but the cancels and numerous corrections in MS seem to have delayed the distribution until the middle of the next year.

HW to Mann, August 1748: 'As my fears about Houghton are great, I am a little pleased to have finished a slight memorial of it, a description of the pictures, of which I have just printed an hundred, to give to particular people: I will send you one, and shall beg Dr. Cocchi to accept another.' 24 October 1748: 'Your brother ... will send them [two copies of *Aedes*] by the first opportunity: I am by no means satisfied with them; they are full of faults, and the two portraits wretchedly unlike.'

HW to Montagu, 5 July 1749: 'He [the Prince of Wales] had seen my *Aedes Walpolianae* at Sir Luke Schaub's, and sent by him to desire one. I sent him one, bound quite in coronation robes....'

Royal quarto; all copies seen are trimmed, and bound in the same mottled calf.
Signatures: A–M⁴; N²; O–Q⁴(Q₄ blank).

Pagination: [i] title-page; [ii] blank; [iii]–vi Dedication to Lord Orford, dated 24 August 1743; vii–xxxv Introduction; [xxxvi] blank; 37–86 Description of Houghton; 87–99 Sermon on Painting, 1742; [100] blank; 101–122 Journey to Houghton, by the Rev. Mr. Whaley; one blank leaf.

Plates: Sir Robert Walpole, frontispiece; Catherine, Lady Walpole, p. 101; two folding plates of floor plans, p. 37; two folding plates showing East and West Fronts, p. 87. The two portraits were engraved by Vertue from miniatures by Zincke.

Cancels: E$_4$, F$_4$, I$_1$ I$_3$, K$_4$, L$_2$

STATES AND VARIANTS

All the lines dividing the fractions in the measurements of pictures are inserted by hand, and small corrections or additions were made fairly regularly in MS by HW in all copies, on the frontispiece, three plates, and some twenty-two pages. But not all the copies have all the corrections, and several corrections noted by HW in his own copy were apparently discovered after he had distributed all or nearly all the copies.

The whole of Signature G exists in two settings of type, and there is a still earlier setting of pp. 49 and 52. The three settings (not mere changes at press but reset pages) can be differentiated and identified by the following points:

Setting 1. Page 49, l. 8, 'Mystake'; l. 20, 'excell'd, are remaakrbly'
Page 52, l. 6, 'Portat'
Page 56, l. 18, '*Carlo*' is misprinted with an inverted *m*, '*warlo*'; corrected in standing type, since the rest of p. 56 is the same as Setting 2.
Pages 50, 51, 53–55 as in Setting 2.

Setting 2. Page 49, l. 8, 'Mistake'; l. 20, 'excell'd, are remarkably'
Page 50, l. 13, 14, 'Saloon' and 'forty wide,' corrected in MS.
Page 52, l. 6, 'Portrait'; 'Virgin' in roman type as in Setting 1.
Page 53, l. 2, 'Mosieur'
Page 56, l. 3 from bottom, 'Another'

Setting 3. Page 49, l. 20, 'excelled, are remarkably'
Page 50, l. 13, 14, 'Salon' and 'thirty wide.'
Page 52, l. 6, 'Virgin' in italic type
Page 53, l. 2, 'Monsieur'
Page 56, l. 3 from bottom, 'another'

HW's copy, now in the Dyce Collection, has the second setting of Signature G. It also preserves the originals of four cancels (I am judging from photostats); they prove chiefly that in 1747 HW had not learned to read proof carefully.

F_4. The cancel leaf was prepared to correct 'The Little Parlour,' on p. 47, to 'The Little Bed-Chamber.'

I_3. The cancel leaf was prepared to correct an absurd error on p. 69, where the Gallery is said to be 'twenty-three' feet long instead of 'seventy-three.' Two smaller errors were corrected on p. 70.

K_4. The cancel leaf was prepared to correct 'the finest Persuasion' on p. 79 to 'the finest Preservation.'

L_2. The cancel leaf was prepared to correct '6 Feet and a half,' at bottom of p. 83, to '3 Feet 6 and a half.' Two smaller errors were corrected on p. 84.

The number of errors seems extraordinary, even in a privately printed volume by an inexperienced author. HW says of it in 'Short Notes,' with disarming casualness: 'It was very incorrectly printed.' The simple truth is that HW, for all his fussy carefulness, had an elegant dilettante's carelessness about details, and he lacked a proof-reader's eye. Gray knew this defect, for he wrote to HW, July 1752: 'Pray, when the fine book [Bentley's *Designs*] is to be printed, let me revise the press, for you know you can't.' And HW refers to Gray's letter, clearly, in a letter to Mason, 15 May 1773: 'I have not the patience necessary for correcting the press. Gray was forever reproaching me with it, and in one of the letters I have just turned over, he says, "Pray send me the proof sheets to correct, for you know you are not capable of it." '

OTHER EDITIONS

The second edition, incorporating numerous corrections and additions in the text and plates, was published by Dodsley, 10 March 1752. Both this and the third edition, and probably the first edition too, were printed by John Hughs, Dodsley's usual printer. The second edition is on slightly smaller paper, A–S⁴, 143 pp., 6 plates.

The book is listed in the *Gentleman's Magazine* for April 1759, but I suppose this to be only Dodsley's attempt to move a small remainder. The third edition, a close reprint of the second, was published in 1767; an uncut copy at Farmington measures approximately 29.4 x 22.5 cm.

Most of the text of HW's description was prefixed to the second

BOOKS BY WALPOLE

edition of Thomas Ripley's *Plans, Elevations and Sections . . . of Houghton,* published by Fourdrinier in 1760. (There is at Farmington a copy of the first edition, 1735, containing a handsome MS copy of HW's description.) HW's text was also included in the first volume of *The English Connoisseur,* 1766, in *The Norfolk Tour,* 1795, and in the second volume of his *Works,* 1798.

Copies

1. HW's MS, carefully written out with undated MS title-page and dedication, including his *Sermon on Painting* but not Whaley's *Journey to Houghton.* Folio magna, illustrated with 120 drawings, prints of portraits at Houghton, etc., as well as plans of buildings; colored drawings by Rubens and Maratti. Original marbled boards, with HW's bookplate inside cover. Directions to the printer in MS laid in; numerous later additions and notes by HW. Listed in *Description of SH,* 1774 and 1784; London Sale, 1842, lot 1124, to Lilly, £14.3.6; offered by Lilly in 1843, and by W. Strong of Bristol, 1843, lot 1881. Purchased in 1925 by Metropolitan Museum, New York.

2. A copy in MS, octavo, calf. Ellis, June 1930, to wsl, £15.15.0.

3. Inscribed on title-page: 'Ex Dono Honoratissimi Eruditissimique Auctoris'; pictures priced in red ink. Signature G in Setting 3. Bookplate of John Towneley, Esq. (1731–1813); it is possible that HW presented the book to Towneley, whom he knew slightly, but perhaps more likely that it came into Towneley's possession somewhat later, since he is not named in HW's list of recipients. Mottled calf, rebacked. Sotheby's, 26 June 1883 (Towneley Hall Sale), lot 2620, to Stewart, 9/–; offered by a bookseller (clipping inserted) for 25/–; from the Gaskill Collection, September 1939, to wsl.

4. Presentation copy to Grosvenor Bedford, inscribed by him; pictures priced in MS. Pencil note by HW pasted on fly-leaf: 'The edition of 1752 is much more ample in the description of this picture of Guido than this edition 1747.' Signature G in Setting 3; final blank wanting. Mottled calf, rebacked. Thorpe, November 1932, to wsl, 35/–.

5. Bookplate of Sir Francis Baring, Bart. (1740–1810), and label of R. W. Chapman. Signature G in Setting 2; final blank wanting. Mottled calf, rebacked. I. K. Fletcher, April 1942, to wsl, £6.6.0.

6. Bookplate removed from inside front cover; Signature G in Setting 1. Mottled calf. Bought by wsl in 1925, 15/–.

7. HW's copy, with his MS additions and corrections and his list of 83 recipients of copies. Signature G in Setting 2. Vellum. SH Sale, iv.155, to Thorpe, £4.4.0; offered by both Thorpe and Longmans in 1842 for £7.7.0; now in the Dyce Collection at South Kensington.

8. Inscribed on title-page: 'Danvers Osborn 1749, Given me by Mr. Horace Walpole.' Mottled calf. Offered by Pickering and Chatto, for £15.15.0 in 1939, for £14 in 1941, and for £15 in 1946.

9. *Second edition,* 1752. HW's copy, with many MS additions and his MS

[31]

catalogue (1736) of the pictures at Houghton inlaid at end, rebound in red morocco by F. Bedford. Possibly the copy listed in SH Sale, vii.45, sold with other volumes to Holloway; offered by Willis in 1855 for £7.10.0; Sotheby's, 7 May 1904 (Ford Sale), lot 642, to Harvey, £15.15.0; now in the Morgan Library.

10. *Third edition*, 1767. HW's copy, bound with a copy of the *Description of SH* 1784, was in SH Sale, vii.41 (London Sale, 1159), to Lilly, £3.19.0 (with Lord Hardwicke's *Walpoliana*); now at Chewton.

5. LETTER TO THE WHIGS. 1747.

'Short Notes': 'About the same time [1747] was published a *Letter to the Tories*, written, as I then believed, by Mr. George Lyttelton. . . . I published an answer to that piece, and called it a *Letter to the Whigs*. It was a careless performance, and written in five days.'

The *Letter to the Tories*, published by Say in June, 1747, is a sixpenny pamphlet of twenty-four pages. It is signed 'J. H.' but the author is not known although the Library of Congress lists Lyttelton as 'supposed author.' The second edition, published in 1748, is a close reprint with a few corrections. HW's copy of the second edition is now at Farmington. HW's reply, being twice as long, was dignified by being priced at one shilling.

In his own copy of the *Second and Third Letter* (see next book), HW again identified Lyttelton as the supposed author of the *Letter to the Tories*, but added: 'After these two *Letters* came out, there was a denial of his being the author printed in a daily paper, but not signed by himself, and it was said that the *Letter to the Tories* was wrote by Dr. Thirlby; but neither of these facts was ever authenticated.'

Octavo in half-sheets; published by Cooper 23 July 1747, at 1/–. An untrimmed copy measures approximately 21.5 x 14 cm.

Signatures: Two leaves unsigned; B–G^4; H^2 (H$_2$ blank).

Pagination: [1] half-title; [2] blank; [3] title-page; [4] blank; 5–54 text; [55–56] blank.

In HW's copy typographical errors on pp. 10, 12, 13, 24, and 37 have been corrected by hand.

EDITIONS

The second edition, published 15 April 1748, is a close reprint of the first; not even the typographical errors are corrected. But by using a smaller type it was compressed to forty pages.

The third edition, published at 1/6 on 27 May 1748, included the *Second and Third Letter* under the title: *Three Letters to the Whigs;*

A LETTER TO THE WHIGS.

OCCASION'D BY

The LETTER to the TORIES.

Quis tulerit Gracchos de Seditione querentes? Juv.

LONDON:
Printed for M. COOPER, at the *Globe* in *Pater-noster-Row.* M.DCC.XLVII.

5.

the Bodleian has a copy. I think the *Letter to the Whigs* has not been reprinted since 1748.

On 25 April 1748, W. Webb published *A Congratulatory Letter to Selim, on the Three Letters to the Whigs*. In May appeared Edward Moore's poem, *The Trial of Selim the Persian*, written to defend Lyttelton (Selim) against various attacks including that by the unknown author of the *Letter to the Whigs*. So it was comic to HW in 1754 that he should be engaged to reconcile Lyttelton and Moore; see HW to Bentley, 18 May 1754.

COPIES

1. HW's copy, bound with *Second and Third Letter* and the second edition of *Letter to the Tories;* numerous identifications by HW. Old mottled calf, with HW's bookplate inside cover; signature 'J. Mitford 1842' on fly-leaf and some notes by Mitford. SH Sale, vii.48 (London Sale 1033), to Payne and Foss, £3.3.0 (with six other volumes); Sotheby's, 24 April 1860 (Mitford Sale), lot 3676, to Booth, £1.8.0; Sotheby's, 25 November 1937 (Newcastle-Clumber Library), lot 911, to Maggs for WSL, £11.

The book is somewhat scarce, but it has never been sought after by collectors. There is a fine uncut copy at Farmington. Three copies are in the British Museum.

6. SECOND AND THIRD LETTER TO THE WHIGS. 1748.

'Short Notes': 'At the end of the year [1747] I wrote two more Letters to the Whigs, but did not publish them till April the next year, when they went through three editions immediately. I had intended to suppress them, but some attacks being made by the Grenvilles on Lord Chief Justice Willes, an intimate friend of my father, . . . I printed them and other pieces.' By 'other pieces' HW no doubt meant the two speeches recorded below.

The Advertisement facing the title-page (and also in the *Daily Advertiser*, 26 March 1748) says that these letters would have been suppressed 'if a late extraordinary attack on the whole Bench of Judges had not convinced the author, that it is necessary to warn his countrymen of what danger their laws and liberties are in, from a certain set of men of the most arbitrary principles.' The letters are said to have been composed four months earlier.

Octavo; published by Cooper, 26 March 1748, at 1/6. An untrimmed copy measures approximately 21.5 x 14 cm.
Signatures: Two leaves unsigned; A–E^8; F^6.
Pagination: Half-title, with Advertisement on verso; title-page, with verso blank; [1]–92 text.

A

SECOND and THIRD

LETTER

TO THE

WHIGS.

By the AUTHOR of the First.

Free as young *Lyttleton* her Caufe purfue.   POPE.

LONDON,
Printed for M. COOPER, at the *Globe* in
Pater-nofter Row.
MDCCXLVIII.

EDITIONS

The second edition is included in the third edition of the first letter, entitled *Three Letters to the Whigs,* published 27 May 1748.

COPIES

The book has never been much sought by collectors, and is about as scarce as the first *Letter*. Harvard, Yale, Columbia, and the New York Public Library have copies, and there are three at Farmington.

7. THE ORIGINAL SPEECH OF SIR WILLIAM STANHOPE. 1748.

In February 1748, the Grenvilles proposed a bill to move the Assizes from Ailesbury to Buckingham as a means of attacking Chief Justice Willes, one of Sir Robert Walpole's friends. HW was anxious to defend his father and planned a speech, but he never delivered it. Instead, he used it for the pamphlet he describes in the next paragraph. (At Farmington there is what seems to be another undelivered speech during the same quarrel.)

'Short Notes': 'During the course of the same bill [the Buckingham Assize Bill], Sir William Stanhope had likewise been interrupted, in a very bitter speech against the Grenvilles. I formed part of the speech I had intended to make, into one for Sir William, and published it in his name. It made great noise. Campbell answered it for a bookseller. I published another, called *The Speech of Richard Whiteliver,* in answer to Campbell's. All these things were only excusable by the lengths to which party had been carried against my father; or rather, were not excusable even then.'

Campbell's reply, published by Moore and reprinted in the *Gentleman's Magazine* for March 1748 and in the *Foundling Hospital for Wit* in 1749, was called: *A Speech without Doors.*

Pot folio; published by Webb, 3 March 1748, at sixpence.
Signatures: One leaf unsigned; B²; C¹.
Pagination: Title-page, with verso blank; [3]–8 text. The title-page was printed with leaf C.

EDITIONS

The speech was reprinted in the *Gentleman's Magazine* for March 1748, in the *London Magazine* for May, and in the sixth number of the *Foundling Hospital for Wit,* 1749. The *Foundling Hospital* copies the misprint in the last sentence, 'presence' for 'preserve,' which the *Gentleman's Magazine* had printed correctly. The speech is also included in the fourteenth volume of the *Parliamentary History.*

THE ORIGINAL

SPEECH

OF

Sir *W——m St——pe*,

On the first reading of the Bill for appointing the Assizes at *Buckingham, Feb.* 19, 1748.

LONDON,
Printed for W. WEBB, near St. *Paul's*, 1748.
[Price Six-pence.]

THE
SPEECH

OF

Richard White-Liver *Esq*;

In behalf of Himself and his Brethren.

Spoken to the most

AUGUST MOB

AT

RAG FAIR.

Hear *Us*, for *We* have been on both Sides.
A new Maxim of our Family.

LONDON,
Printed for W. WEBB, near St. *Paul*'s, 1748.
⌜ Price SIX-PENCE. ⌝
8. REDUCED. WIDTH OF ORIGINAL 13.2 CM.

Copies

The only copy I have seen is almost uncut, in a modern wrapper; purchased by WSL from Swift in August 1936.

8. THE SPEECH OF RICHARD WHITELIVER. 1748.

See 'Short Notes' under *The Original Speech of Sir William Stanhope* immediately above.

Pot folio; published by Webb in March 1748, at sixpence.
Signatures: Two sheets, quired, the second leaf signed B.
Pagination: [1] title-page; [2] blank; [3]–7 text; [8] blank.

Editions

The speech was reprinted in the sixth number of the *Foundling Hospital for Wit*, 1749; punctuation and capitalization are altered freely, but the only significant change is the word 'disposed' which was correctly printed 'deposed' in the original.

Copies

The only copy I have seen is at the University of Illinois, heavily trimmed, bound in a quarto volume of pamphlets; it was acquired from Blackwell's of Oxford in 1942.

9. A LETTER FROM XO HO. 1757.

HW to George Grenville, 13 May 1757: 'The ridiculous situation of this country for some months drew from me yesterday the enclosed thoughts, which I beg you will be so good as to run over and return.'

MS note by HW in his own copy of the first edition: 'Written 12 May 1757; printed May 17 and a second edition on the 20th.'

'Short Notes': 'May 12th of that year [1757], I wrote in less than an hour and a half the *Letter from Xo Ho;* it was published on the 17th, and immediately passed through five editions.'

HW to Montagu, 2 June 1757: 'I don't know how you came not to see the advertisements of *Xo Ho,* which have been in continually; four editions were published in twelve days.'

There is no real contradiction between HW's two remarks about the success of his little satire. The first edition was perhaps available on 17 May, although the first advertisements (in the *Daily Advertiser* and the *London Evening Post*) appeared on the 19th. The second edition was advertised 20 May; the third edition, 24 May; and the fourth edition, 31 May, just twelve days after the advertisement of the first edition. The fifth edition was published 27 June, six

A LETTER

FROM

XO HO, a *Chinese* Philosopher at LONDON,

TO HIS FRIEND

LIEN CHI at *PEKING*.

By Horace Walpole.

LONDON:

Printed for N. MIDDLETON, in the *Strand*.

(Price Sixpence.)

9. REDUCED. WIDTH OF ORIGINAL 12.8 cm.

weeks after the first edition. But when HW printed his *Fugitive Pieces* a year later, he wrote somewhat carelessly: 'This piece was written 12 May 1757, was sent to the press next day, and went through five editions in a fortnight.'

Austin Dobson and others have pointed out that HW's Lien Chi is strangely like Lien Chi Altangi, and there seems no reason to doubt that Goldsmith picked up the name from HW's satire, which was given a short but favorable notice in the *Monthly Review* for May 1757. A more direct reply was published 20 June: *An answer from Lien Chi in Pekin, to Xo Ho the Chinese philosopher in London, to which is annexed a letter from Philo-Briton to Lien Chi.* The *Monthly Review* was very scornful of this reply.

Foolscap folio; approximately 33.5 x 21 cm. uncut; price sixpence.
Signatures: Two sheets, quired; inner sheet signed B.
Pagination: Title-page, with verso blank; 1–6 text.

STATES AND VARIANTS

The *Gentleman's Magazine, Critical Review,* and *Monthly Review* all record the publisher as Graham. All copies of the first edition seem to have N. Middleton as publisher. Copies of the first edition were sold with such unexpected speed, apparently, that the second edition published three days later by Graham had to be used for review copies. I do not know why there should have been a change in publishers. Graham was associated with Bathoe, HW's bookseller; possibly Middleton was also linked to Bathoe.

Perhaps more interesting than the change of publishers is the fact that all five editions were printed from standing type. In the second edition, the title-page carries the added words 'The Second Edition,' and the publisher's name is changed, but I cannot find any change in the text. The imprint is changed again slightly in the fourth edition, but the text is printed from the same type in all five editions. All editions are undated.

OTHER EDITIONS

In addition to the series of five editions in folio, HW's *Letter to Xo Ho* was reprinted in his *Fugitive Pieces,* 1758, and in the collected *Works* in quarto. A considerable extract was reprinted in the *London Chronicle,* 2 June 1757.

COPIES

1. HW's copy, with his annotations, and notice from the *Critical Review*; uncut and unbound. Mrs. Bentley, March 1937, to WSL, in a collection.

2. Two other copies of the first edition are at Farmington, and one at Harvard. Two copies of the second edition are at Harvard, and one copy each at Farmington and at Yale. The British Museum has a copy of the third edition. George Chetwynd's copy of the fourth edition, in a volume of tracts, is at Harvard; and the Library of Congress has a copy of the fourth edition. Harvard and the British Museum have copies of the fifth edition.

10. CATALOGUE OF ROYAL AND NOBLE AUTHORS. 1758.

For description see *SH Bibliography,* pp. 33–37, 87–94 *(Works),* and 135–36 *(Postscript).*

On p. 36 the record of an edition dated 1763 is a ghost and should be deleted. I made it, carelessly, from a Library of Congress card, but the card was made by a careless misreading of the Roman numerals of the SH edition.

Of Thomas Park's edition in five volumes, 1806, I may add that copies were imposed both in octavo and in quarto, the latter producing a few handsome large-paper copies. In one copy of the octavo, I have found the preliminary leaves reset in all volumes, although the watermark (1805) is the same as in other copies. Many of the plates are dated 1 February 1807, and the edition was not published until late in 1807. Proofs of the plates were formerly much sought by collectors. In most copies of the fifth volume leaf D_2 (F_2 in the quarto) and leaf L_8 (X_4 in the quarto) are cancels.

The set of Park's edition in the Library of Congress has a new title-page in the third volume dated 1812; in a copy at Farmington containing advertisements dated 1814, the title-pages of the second and third volumes have been reprinted (watermarked 1811), although 1806 is kept in the imprint; in a copy at the University of California, the title-pages of the second and third volumes are dated 1812. I have not seen the reissue *(ca.* 1823) described in *Notes and Queries,* 3d Series, vi.283 (1864) and recorded in Lowndes and in the *Dictionary of National Biography* under 'Park': it appears to have contained a new paragraph in the editor's preface, several cancels, and HW's appendix that was still protected by copyright in 1806.

11. FUGITIVE PIECES. 1758.

For description see *SH Bibliography,* p. 39.

The following pieces were first published in this volume:

(1) 'Verses in Memory of King Henry the Sixth,' written at Cambridge, 2 February 1738. HW's transcript in the *Waldegrave MS* shows that he made some small revisions before printing in 1758. The verses were reprinted in the first volume of the *New Foundling Hospital for Wit,* 1784.

(2) 'Inscription for the Neglected Column in the Place of St. Mark at Florence,' written in 1740. HW's transcript in the *Waldegrave MS* has an earlier text, somewhat closer to that sent by HW to Spence in 1751 (MS now at Huntington Library; printed in Spence's *Anecdotes,* 1820, p. 440). The inscription was re-

printed in the *Annual Register* for 1772, and in the first volume of the *New Foundling Hospital for Wit*, 1784.

(3) 'The Entail,' written in 1754. See 'Short Notes': 'In July of that year [1754] I wrote "The Entail," a fable in verse.' It was reprinted in the *Annual Register* for 1772, and in the first volume of the *New Foundling Hospital for Wit*, 1784. A copy of the poem in HW's hand, formerly in the Waller Collection, is now WSL. HW's transcript of the poem is in the *Waldegrave MS*. In the twelfth number of 'Miscellaneous Antiquities' in 1936, *Bentley's Designs for Walpole's Fugitive Pieces*, Mr. Lewis published Bentley's drawings for 'The Entail.'

(4) 'Epigram on Admiral Vernon, 1750.' It was reprinted in the first volume of the *New Foundling Hospital for Wit*, 1784. HW's transcript is in the *Waldegrave MS*.

(5) 'Epitaph on the Cenotaph of Lady Walpole erected . . . in July 1754.' To his transcript in the *Waldegrave MS* HW added this note: 'This epitaph was written at Florence in 1740. . . . Lady Walpole is buried at Houghton in Norfolk.' An early copy in HW's autograph is at the Liverpool Public Library.

(6) Supplementary account of Theodore of Corsica.

(7) Two numbers of *The World*, not used in the periodical. The MSS are now at Farmington; see Contributions to Periodicals below.

(8) An inquiry into the person and age of the long-lived Countess of Desmond.

(9) Inscription on a picture of the late Pope.

All these pieces were included when the *Fugitive Pieces* were reprinted in the *Works* of 1770 and 1798. The poetical pieces were reprinted by WSL in 1931 in his collection of *HW's Fugitive Verses*.

12. DIALOGUE BETWEEN TWO GREAT LADIES. 1760.

'Short Notes': '13 March [1760], wrote the *Dialogue between Two Great Ladies*. It was published 23 April, being deferred till after the trials of Lord G. Sackville and Lord Ferrers.'

HW's delay in publishing this short satire on the German war until after Lord George Sackville's trial can be explained by a passage on p. 15 in which Maria Theresa says: 'Your ideas are very romantic. The English, whom you admire, do not push their generosity so far. Did not they lately put an admiral [Byng] to death, for supposing he had beaten the French when he had not?' Throughout the *Dialogue*, the letters M. T. stand for Maria Theresa, and E. for the Empress of Russia.

The *Monthly Review* was not greatly impressed by the book; it pointed out that the author's main design was to show that it was not for England's advantage to have a little territory in Germany.

Small octavo in half-sheets; published 23 April 1760 at sixpence by M. Cooper.
Signatures: One leaf unsigned; A–B⁴; one leaf unsigned.
Pagination: [1] title-page; [2] blank; 3–19 text; [20] blank.

A
DIALOGUE
BETWEEN
Two Great Ladies.

LONDON:
Printed for M. COOPER, in Pater-noster-row.
MDCCLX.
(PRICE SIX-PENCE.)
12.

BOOKS BY WALPOLE

COPIES

HW's copy, rebound, is in the Library of King's College, Cambridge. I have examined only a copy acquired in 1897 by the New York Public Library; it is now bound in a volume of miscellaneous pamphlets.

13. CATALOGUE OF PICTURES AND DRAWINGS IN THE HOLBEIN CHAMBER. 1760.

For description see *SH Bibliography,* p. 50.

14. ANECDOTES OF PAINTING. 1762–71.

For description see *SH Bibliography,* p. 50.

Two errors in my record of copies may properly be corrected here. On p. 68, Copy 3 of the second edition was acquired by wsL at the Hartshorne Sale, 30 October 1945, for $210. It is extra-illustrated and extensively annotated by Thomas Kirgate, and it includes the *Additional Lives to complete* [Vol. 2 of] *the first Edition,* as well as the cancelled Advertisement (1773) to Vol. 4, and other materials. The binding of this set (green morocco gilt, with joints, by C. Smith) is identical with that of Copy 1; and it was certainly this set, not Copy 1, that was sold at Christie's in 1892 for £48. On p. 66, Copy 1 of the first edition (at the Morgan Library) was described as containing MS notes by HW; Mr. Lewis is convinced that the notes are not by HW but merely copies in another hand.

At the bottom of p. 65, the *Catalogue of Engravers* of 1794 had, on the original title-page, the imprint: Printed by J. Moore, for J. Caulfield, T. Coram, and G. Barrett; copies exist with a new title-page: Printed for Eglin and Pepys. (See *Notes and Queries,* 1862, 3d Series, ii.350.) On p. 66: Dallaway's edition of 1826–28, originally published at ten guineas, or fifteen guineas for sets on large paper with India proofs of the plates, was remaindered by Bohn after Major's bankruptcy for four and five guineas, respectively. Sets with proof plates were formerly much sought by collectors.

15. THE OPPOSITION TO THE LATE MINISTER VINDICATED. 1763.

On 8 April 1763 Lord Bute resigned unexpectedly; there seems no doubt that his reasons were at least in part those attributed to him by the Opposition: the dissatisfaction of Pitt and other leaders with the peace treaty concluded on 10 February 1763, and the violent popular and Parliamentary outcry against the new excise on cider forced through Parliament at the end of March.

On 12 May 1763 Becket published Owen Ruffhead's anonymous pamphlet, *Considerations on the present dangerous Crisis,* of which a second edition was published 17 May and a third edition 2 June. The *Monthly Review* spoke

THE OPPOSITION

To the Late

MINISTER VINDICATED

From the Aspersions of a PAMPHLET, intitled,

CONSIDERATIONS

ON THE PRESENT

DANGEROUS CRISIS.

LONDON:
Printed for W. BATHOE near *Exeter-Change* in the *Strand*.

MDCCLXIII.

favorably of the work, not unexpectedly, since Ruffhead was a staff reviewer; and the *London Chronicle* and *Gentleman's Magazine* quoted long extracts from it. HW's copy (of the second edition) has no annotation beyond the date 'May' on the title-page.

When the reply to Ruffhead, *The Opposition to the late Minister Vindicated,* was published early in June, it was noticed somewhat condescendingly in the *Monthly Review,* but long extracts from it were quoted prominently in the *Gentleman's Magazine* for June.

There seems enough evidence to suggest that this reply was written by HW.

(1) John Almon, in his *Biographical, Literary, and Political Anecdotes,* published late in 1797 (i.45) asserts that HW wrote it 'in the autumn of 1763.' He is not exact about the time of year, but his evidence may be accurate in other respects. In 1763 Almon was busily engaged in writing political pamphlets, particularly as a supporter of Wilkes; he compiled the *History of the late Minority* (1765), the *Review of Mr. Pitt's Administration* (November 1762), and (in April and May 1763) the *Review of Lord Bute's Administration.* It is not astonishing that Ruffhead wrote a violent condemnation of the last-named pamphlet for the *Monthly Review* in June; but Almon had access to much important information, and all these compilations contain many accurate facts along with minor errors. Furthermore, Almon published for HW in 1764 his *Counter-Address to the Public* (see the next entry in the *Bibliography*). Almon, therefore, was perhaps as likely as any man to know the authorship of anonymous pamphlets on the Whig side, and as publisher to HW the next year he might easily have learned about this particular one. I can see no incentive for him to falsify his evidence in 1797, just after HW's death, and despite his limitations he is sufficiently reliable to be a respectable witness.

(2) In a note for Richard Bull (MS now in the Huntington Library), Thomas Kirgate listed three 'Pieces, by Horace Walpole Earl of Orford, not inserted in his Works.' The three are: *Reflections on Cruelty,* Tonson, 1759 [only the dedication is by HW, but Kirgate is correct in recording the item]; *The Opposition to the late Minister Vindicated,* Bathoe, 1763; *A Counter-Address to the Public,* Almon, 1764 [Kirgate records the fourth edition]. Since the *Counter-Address* is printed in the *Works* of 1798, Kirgate's note is certainly earlier than that; since he does not say 'the late Horace Walpole,' the note is almost certainly earlier than March 1797, and more likely to be soon after December 1791 when HW succeeded as Earl of Orford. The establishment of the date of the note is important, because Kirgate's evidence is thus proved to be independent, not derived from Almon's *Biographical Anecdotes.* Kirgate was right on the other two pamphlets, and from 1765 to 1797 he was in an excellent position to learn about the *Opposition Vindicated,* either from his employer when they began printing his collected *Works* or from Bathoe before the latter's death in 1768.

(3) Bibliographically, the evidence is slighter but confirmatory. So far as I know, this is the only political pamphlet published by Bathoe, in a period when

certain booksellers were publishing dozens of them. But Bathoe had a working partnership with Graham who published HW's *Letter from Xo Ho* in 1757, as well as Whitworth's *Russia* in 1758 and the second edition of *Royal and Noble Authors* in 1759; he was the publisher of HW's Vertue *Catalogues* (Charles I, James II, Duke of Buckingham) in 1757–59, of the *Anecdotes of Painting* in 1762–67, and of the *Castle of Otranto* in 1765. Thus Bathoe was HW's regular publisher (Dodsley handled the sales of the SH Lucan, and M. Cooper published the anonymous *Dialogue between Two Great Ladies* in 1760) from 1757 to 1763, and in a letter to David Dalrymple, 31 January 1764, HW speaks of 'my publisher Bathoe.' In addition Bathoe was HW's agent in August 1763 in some dealings with the printer William Pratt (see HW's *Journal of the Printing Office*, 1923, p. 85; and the memorandum by HW on Montagu's letter of 27 September 1763, printed in the Yale edition, ii.102). And the Bathoe-Graham firm was HW's agent at Dr. Mead's sale (see HW to Bentley, 13 December 1754), and probably at many other auctions. For Bathoe, who published no other political pamphlets, to publish this one anonymously for his client HW seems very natural; and the secret of authorship could be considered safe with Bathoe. Of course HW was anxious not to be known as the author, inasmuch as Lord Bute, with whom he wanted to appear to be on good terms, was still in power.

(4) The *Opposition Vindicated* was included uncritically as HW's in Bohn's revision of Lowndes. More importantly, it was accepted without question by A. T. Bartholomew, a careful bibliographer, in the *Cambridge History of English Literature* (the bibliography for Chap. 17 of Vol. X), 1913.

(5) Stylistically, the answer to his opponent point by point seems to me quite in the manner of the *Counter-Address* of 1764, as does the device of picking out particular words or phrases for emphasis. Mr. Lewis points out that the phrase 'affectation of candour' is characteristically Walpolian. The essay seems also to have been written by somebody who knew the Parliamentary debates at first hand: Ruffhead had asserted that the Cider Tax passed the Commons without a division, and no ordinary reader of the newspapers could know the exact history of the debate; but the author of the *Opposition Vindicated* knows the details, for he writes: 'What shall we say to a writer [Ruffhead] of decency and apparent authority, who ventures to assert an absolute falsehood, which this gentleman does in saying that the bill passed through the House of Commons without a division. I would not in direct terms charge him with a falsehood if I could not appeal to every member of that honourable House, whether there were not at least *six* divisions upon it.' Clearly the writer of those sentences was a member, or he had exactly reliable first-hand information from a member.

Furthermore, HW was seriously distressed by Lord Bute's high-handed redistribution of patent-reversions. See his *Memoirs of George III*, 1845, i.265: 'The reversion of Auditor of the Imprest was obtained for his own son Lord Mount-Stewart. My place of Usher of the Exchequer was granted in reversion to Samuel Martin; and a place in the Custom-house, held by my brother, . . . was also granted in reversion to Jenkinson. I was, I confess, much provoked at this

[48]

BOOKS BY WALPOLE

last grant, and took occasion of fomenting the ill-humour against the favourite, who thus excluded me from the possibility of obtaining the continuance of that place to myself in case of my brother's death.' In a letter to Montagu, 14 April 1763, HW details much the same facts. Such an attitude seems to me to fit the following comment, near the end of the *Opposition Vindicated:* 'Some late proceedings impress no very high idea of their ability, and certain pensions and reversionary patents which have been talked of in this dawn of their administration, and have not been absolutely denied, render their disinterestedness very doubtful.'

Indeed, HW's phrase just quoted from his *Memoirs*, 'I was, I confess, much provoked at this last grant, and took occasion of fomenting the ill-humour against the favourite,' seems most easily explicable if he wrote anonymously to the newspapers—or if he wrote anonymously just such a pamphlet as the *Opposition Vindicated*.

(6) It is proper to consider the evidence against HW's authorship. The *Opposition Vindicated* is not in the *Works* of 1798; but neither are the *Letters to the Whigs* and his other inflammatory writings of 1748. It is not mentioned in 'Short Notes'; but neither is the *Description of SH*, 1774. There are, I think, no references in extant letters that could fit this pamphlet. But he was extremely anxious to be undetected, just as he was in 1773 when he was careful to make it appear in all his letters that he did not know Mason to be the author of the *Heroic Epistle*. (On his own copy of the *Heroic Epistle,* now Harvard, HW wrote the month of publication but not the author's name.)

The copy of the *Opposition Vindicated* at Columbia is inscribed: 'Nic. Bonfoy. An Excellent Pamphlet. By Dr. B-tl-r.' But I think Bonfoy, not notable as a bibliographer, confused HW's tract with one of similar title by John Butler, Bishop of Hereford: *Serious considerations on the measures of the present administration,* 1763. Dr. Butler's tract was published by Kearsley, and I think perhaps Bonfoy merely confused the gossip he had heard about that with the anonymous tract he had bought.

It would be pleasant to find that HW owned a copy, with his authorship established by a MS note. But he seems to have owned no copy, at least not in the collection of tracts in which he preserved Ruffhead's pamphlet. Yet I do not know that his failure to own a copy is a serious objection. He must have known about the book, since it was prominently displayed in the *Gentleman's Magazine* and since his agent Bathoe was the publisher. If he kept a copy at all, it was in some unidentified volume of tracts; if he intentionally kept no copy, his action would not be wholly inexplicable in an author who was anxious to remain genuinely anonymous. HW was anxious to remain on superficially friendly terms with Lord Bute, and he could not have hoped to do so, had the slightest rumor been circulated that he was the author of this attack.

Some conclusive evidence of HW's authorship may appear at any time. For the present, if my interpretation of the available evidence is correct, the *Opposition Vindicated* will have to be counted as 'probably by HW.'

Octavo; published early in June 1763 by Bathoe, at 1/–.
Signatures: A–C⁸ (C₈ blank).
Pagination: [1] half-title; [2] blank; [3] title-page; [4] blank; [5]–45 text; [46–48] blank.

COPIES

It is difficult to tell how rare the book is, since it has never been sought after. There is no copy at Farmington, but there are copies at Chicago and Columbia, two at the British Museum, and three at Yale.

16. A COUNTER-ADDRESS TO THE PUBLIC. 1764.

'Short Notes': '29 May 1764. Began an answer to a pamphlet against Mr. Conway, called *An Address to the Public on the late Dismission of a General Officer.* My answer was finished June 12th, but not published till August 2nd, under the title of *A Counter-Address to the Public, &c.*'

The *Address to the Public,* to which HW replied, was by William Guthrie. In September Guthrie published his own reply to HW, under the title, *A Reply to the Counter-Address.* HW's copy of Guthrie's *Address,* with one MS note, is bound in his *Collection of Tracts,* just before his own pamphlet.

Octavo in half-sheets; published 2 August, at one shilling, by J. Almon.
It was advertised as also 'sold by J. Williams,' one of the publishers of the *North Briton.*
Signatures: A, C–G⁴.
Pagination: [1] title-page; [2] blank; [3]–47 text; [48] advertisements.

EDITIONS

Four editions were published in rapid succession, from standing type, all on the same kind of paper. The first edition was published 2 August, and the second 9 August, without change. In the third edition, advertised as published 16 August, the sequence of signatures was normalized (A–F⁴) and two small corrections were made in the text ('Action' *to* 'Act' on p. 7, and 'Officer' *to* 'Author' on p. 13). The fourth edition was published 1 September, without change.

The pamphlet was reprinted in the first volume of Almon's *Collection of scarce and interesting tracts,* 1787; and in the second volume of HW's *Works,* 1798. Extracts from it were included in a sketch of Conway's career in the *Public Advertiser,* 3 April 1782.

A COUNTER-ADDRESS TO THE PUBLIC,

ON THE

LATE DISMISSION

OF A

GENERAL OFFICER.

By Mr Horace Walpole.

Henri voit pres des Rois leurs insolens ministres:
Il remarque sur tout ces conseillers sinistres,
Qui des moeurs & des loix avares corrupteurs,
De Themis & de Mars ont vendu les honneurs:
Qui mirent les premiers à d'indignes encheres,
L'inestimable prix des vertus de nos peres.

HENRIADE, Chant. vii.

LONDON:
Printed for J. ALMON, opposite *Burlington-House* in *Piccadilly*. 1764.
[Price One Shilling.]

16.

COPIES

1. HW's copy, with the title-page inscribed 'By Mr. Horace Walpole' and dated August 2d, is in his *Collection of Tracts of George III*, Volume 8, now WSL. The collection is recorded in the *SH Bibliography*, p. 255. The pages of this copy contain a few corrections and annotations.

17. THE CASTLE OF OTRANTO. 1765.

HW told William Cole, in his letter of 9 March 1765, that he began his story, under the inspiration of a dream, at the beginning of June, 1764.

'Short Notes': 'June [1764]. I began *The Castle of Otranto,* a Gothic story, and finished it August 6th. . . . December 24, *The Castle of Otranto* was published; 500 copies. . . . April 11, 1765. The second edition of *The Castle of Otranto;* 500 copies.'

Although the first edition was published a week before the end of the year, all copies are dated 1765.

The assertion on the title-page that the story was written by Onuphrio Muralto is properly recorded as a literary hoax, not a forgery, since HW admitted his authorship as soon as the book succeeded. His disingenuous preface to the first edition, in which he asserted that he, William Marshall, was translating from a rare Italian volume printed in 1529, was perhaps planned as a shield against the scoffing and scornful, and it has done the world little harm. (See HW to William Cole, 28 February 1765: '. . . a little story-book, which I published some time ago, though not boldly with my own name; but it has succeeded so well, that I do not any longer entirely keep the secret.' Many years earlier, 3 November 1746, he had written Montagu about his Epilogue to *Tamerlane,* saying: 'I have kept secret whose it is.')

Octavo; published 24 December 1764 by T. Lownds at 3/–; the copies I have examined have been trimmed by the binder.

Signatures: A⁴; B–N⁸; O⁴.

Pagination: [i] title-page; [ii] blank; [iii]–viii The Translator's Preface; [1]–200 text.

COPIES

1. HW's copy, calf, with his arms on sides; SH Sale, iv.166, to Thorpe, £3.10.0 (with second edition); Sotheby's, 27 March 1857 (Utterson Sale), lot 1697, to Nattali, £4.

2. William Cole's copy, with his bookplate and with his name on title-page (reproduced in Yale Edition of HW's *Correspondence,* i.85); Cole has corrected a few errors and transcribed on the fly-leaf some extracts from HW's letters to him and George Birch's commendatory verses; in 1774 Cole added a note about the dedicatory verses to Lady Mary Coke which HW had printed in the second edition. Inscribed on fly-leaf: 'Hester Barnardiston. This book was a present from

THE
Castle of Otranto,
A
STORY.

Translated by

WILLIAM MARSHAL, Gent.

From the Original ITALIAN of

ONUPHRIO MURALTO,

CANON of the Church of St. NICHOLAS
at OTRANTO.

LONDON:
Printed for THO. LOWNDS in Fleet-Street.
MDCCLXV.

the Revd. Mr. Cole of Milton who received it from the author. 1777.' (Cole's friend, John Barnardiston [d. 1778], was Master of Corpus Christi College; his wife died in 1770, and this Hester is probably their only child.) Rebound in modern blue morocco by Rivière and Son. Maggs, May 1925, to WSL, £16.

3. Richard Bull's copy, with his bookplate and inscription; rebound by Bull in red morocco; water-color of the Castle, copied from one made in Italy in 1785 by Reveley, mounted by Bull on fly-leaf. Sotheby's, 27 June 1894 (Julia Swinburne Sale), lot 4, to Walford, 8/–; Scribner's, December 1937, to WSL, $250.

4. Charles Bedford's copy, red morocco, with his cipher on spine and his bookplate. Sotheby's, 12 April 1938 (Miscellaneous Sale), lot 300, to Scribner's, £31.

OTHER EDITIONS

The Castle of Otranto is perhaps more interesting in some of its later editions than in the first edition. In the total number of editions the book has displayed a rather astonishing vitality; I have included here the date and any identifying features of the uninteresting editions, pausing for more complete collation of Bodoni's edition of 1791 and the Italian translation printed at London in 1795. The list after 1800 is certainly not complete, but I include such editions as have come to my attention. It was also included in HW's *Works*.

An abridgment, published serially in the *Universal Magazine* for 1765, seems to have no distinction other than its prompt appearance.

Dublin, 1765. Printed for Elizabeth Watts; duodecimo. This edition was reprinted from the text of the first London edition.

Dublin, 1765. Printed for J. Hoey [etc.]; duodecimo in half-sheets. This was also reprinted from the text of the first London edition, but two typographical errors were corrected.

Second edition, London, 1765. 'Printed for William Bathoe and Thomas Lownds'; octavo. This edition is a page-for-page reprint of the first edition, but typographical errors are corrected and HW added a Sonnet to Lady Mary Coke and a long Preface to the Second Edition in which he acknowledged his authorship of the book. It collates A–N^8; O^4. In the new Preface, the name of Guildenstern's double is misprinted 'Rosencraus,' an error that persisted through half a dozen editions. HW's attack on Voltaire in this Preface was not necessary, but I have little doubt that he enjoyed writing it; his several comments quoted herewith indicate that he had no desire to stir up a quarrel with Voltaire:

'Paris Journals': '31 October 1765. Mme. du Deffand desired me to lend him [Florian] *The Castle of Otranto* to translate; I did not care it should be translated; besides, the preface to second edition is writ against his uncle Voltaire. I said I would lend it him if he would not translate it, and determined to show only first edition.' (*Correspondence with Madame du Deffand,* Yale ed., 1939, v.269.)

'Short Notes': '20 June 1768. Received a letter from Voltaire desiring my *Historic Doubts.* I sent them, and *The Castle of Otranto,* that he might see the preface of which I told him. . . .'

HW to Voltaire, 21 June 1768: 'Some time ago I took the liberty to find fault in print with the criticisms you had made on our Shakespeare. . . . It was in a preface to a trifling romance, much unworthy of your regard, but which I shall send you. . . . I might retract, I might beg your pardon; but having said nothing but what I thought, . . . it would be treating you with ingratitude and impertinence, to suppose that you would either be offended with my remarks, or pleased with my recantation.'

Lord Dacre's copy of the second edition (now WSL) and a presentation copy from HW to Thomas Percy (now Yale) have the title-page and preface to the first edition bound in after the new preface, an interesting way of showing HW's two attitudes toward the book. Percy wrote an inscription in his copy, on the verso of the title-page to the first edition, and dated it 15 March 1765: possibly he wrote in error for 15 April, although advance copies of the second edition may have been ready well before the date of publication, 11 April; or perhaps it is more likely that HW gave Percy the first edition in March (he gave Cole a copy early in March), that Percy then inscribed it, and later saved only the preliminaries to put with a copy of the corrected second edition.

HW's copy of the second edition, bound in calf with his arms on sides, with drawings and engravings inserted and a long MS note by HW, was sold at the SH Sale, iv.166, with the first edition. It was acquired by E. V. Utterson, and was sold at Sotheby's, 27 March 1857 (Utterson Sale), lot 1698, to Leyton, £7.17.6; it reappeared at Sotheby's in 1870 (Corser Sale), lot 944, and was sold to Boone, £4.10.0.

Third edition, London, 1766. Printed for William Bathoe; octavo. In this edition, both prefaces were included, as they were generally in succeeding editions. After Bathoe's death in 1768, the sheets of this edition were taken over by John Murray and reissued with a cancel title-page marked 'Third edition' and dated 1769. It was one of the first books published by Murray.

French translation by Marc Antoine Eidous, Amsterdam and Paris,

1767; two volumes, duodecimo. This appears to be the first edition with HW's name on the title-page. HW recorded it in 'Short Notes': 'March 1767. A bad translation of *The Castle of Otranto* into French was published at Paris this month.'

HW's copy was listed in SH Sale, vii.33, but it is not clearly indicated in the recataloguing for the London Sale in June, 1842; it was offered in T. Thorpe's *General Cat.*, 1845, Part II, lot 5132, 5/–.

Fourth edition, London, 1782. Printed for James Dodsley; octavo. A page-for-page reprint of the third edition.

HW's copy, with his signature and bookplate, bound with a presentation copy of Jephson's *Count of Narbonne*, Dublin 1782, was bought at George Daniel's Sale in 1864 by Harvey, £1.15.0. It was owned in 1936 by Mrs. Scott-Murray of Heckfield. It is not certainly identifiable in the SH Sale.

Fifth edition, London, Dodsley, 1786. Octavo.

Sixth edition, London, Dodsley, 1791. Octavo. This reprint of the fifth edition is sometimes referred to as the edition on small paper, to differentiate it from Bodoni's handsome edition next described.

Sixth edition, Parma, 1791. Printed by Bodoni for James Edwards of London; quarto. This edition is enough of a collector's item to justify a detailed description. The project was conceived and paid for by Edwards, with HW's approval.

Extracts of the Journals and Correspondence of Miss Berry, ed. Lady Theresa Lewis, 1865, i.242: '8 November 1790. . . . At the printing-office [Bodoni's in Parma] they go on very slowly, but their work is excellent: they had just finished an impression of three hundred copies of the *Castle of Otranto*, for Edwards the bookseller in London, and five copies upon vellum. With the director (Bodoni), who seems to be a clever man and fond of his art, I had a good deal of conversation in a bookseller's shop.'

HW to Agnes Berry, 28 November 1790: 'I am sorry the bookseller [i.e., Bodoni] would not let you have an *Otranto*. Edwards told me, above two months ago, that he every day expected the whole impression; and he has never mentioned it waiting for my corrections. I will make Kirgate write to him.'

HW to Mary Berry, 20 December 1790: 'I am glad you did not get a Parmesan *Otranto*. A copy is come so full of faults, that it is not fit to be sold here.' The bibliographical evidence presented below makes it clear that HW ordered such extensive corrections, that the publication was delayed to enable Bodoni to prepare cancels.

James Edwards to HW, 21 October 1791: '*The Castle of Otranto* is at length arrived, and I have sent you the first we have yet got done up—as soon as they are bound I will do myself the honor to wait upon you with a few others.'

Quarto; an uncut copy measures approximately 25.5 x 17.5 cm.
Signatures: Four leaves unsigned (first blank); 1–4⁴; a–hh⁴(hh₄ blank).
Pagination: One blank leaf; half-title, with verso blank; title-page, with motto on verso; George Birch's verses, with verso blank; [i]–xi Preface to first edition; [xii] blank; xiii Sonnet to Lady Mary Coke; [xiv] blank; xv–xxxii Preface to second edition; [1]–245 text; [246–248] blank.
Cancels: a₂, b₄, c₃, d₁, d₄, e₁, f₃, h₃, m₃, n₂, y₂, z₂. In addition, the title-page is a cancel, and the first sheet of the Preface and the last two sheets of the text are reprinted on the same paper as that used for the cancels. Because the title-page is a cancel, the conjugate half-title is rather frequently missing in bound copies.

STATES AND VARIANTS

The uncancelled leaves are preserved in the Huntington Library's copy on vellum (and no doubt in any other copies that preserve the earlier title-page dated 1790). It is clear that HW must have read the text in December 1790 with some care: each cancel corrects one or more typographical errors caused by the printer's lack of familiarity with English. Many awkward divisions of words ('sou-/ght' and 'so-/me' on p. 33, for example) are corrected, and glaring misprints like 'loked' for 'locked' on p. 25. As might be expected, the printer introduced a number of new errors when he reset the type for the cancels; and it is hardly necessary to add that similar errors can be found uncorrected on other, uncancelled leaves.

Since some other pages near the end, although not cancels in any copy, have a different setting of type in the Huntington copy, it seems possible that the copies on vellum were printed first and some changes were then made before any copy was sent to England.

Lowndes, who describes the Parma edition as octavo, records some copies on large paper, and various copies have been so described in auction catalogues ever since the Roxburghe Sale in 1812. It is true that the Parma edition is occasionally described by booksellers as large paper merely to differentiate it from Dodsley's octavo of 1791 listed above; but to describe a copy as the large-paper issue of the

THE CASTLE
OF OTRANTO,
A
GOTHIC STORY.

TRANSLATED

BY

WILLIAM MARSHAL, GENT.

FROM THE ORIGINAL ITALIAN

OF ONUPHRIO MURALTO,

CANON OF THE CHURCH OF ST. NICHOLAS

AT OTRANTO.

THE SIXTH EDITION.

PRINTED

WITH BODONI'S CHARACTERS

FOR EDWARDS BOOKSELL.R OF LONDON

MDCCXC

FIRST STATE OF BODONI'S TITLE-PAGE.

THE CASTLE
OF OTRANTO,
A
GOTHIC STORY.

TRANSLATED
BY
WILLIAM MARSHAL, GENT.
FROM THE ORIGINAL ITALIAN
OF ONUPHRIO MURALTO,
CANON OF THE CHURCH OF ST. NICHOLAS
AT OTRANTO.

THE SIXTH EDITION.

PARMA.
PRINTED BY BODONI, FOR
J. EDWARDS, BOOKSELLER OF LONDON.
MDCCXCI.

SECOND STATE OF BODONI'S TITLE-PAGE.

Parma edition is certainly an error. Miss Berry speaks precisely of an edition of three hundred copies and five on vellum, with no reference to any on large paper. All copies I have seen are on the same Italian paper, printed in quarto although the dimensions resemble those of an English royal octavo. It is therefore easy to look at a single copy, note that it is apparently a royal octavo, and believe that it is one of the large-paper copies recorded by Lowndes: I have notes of several copies described as royal or imperial octavo, large paper. But even HW's copy, though it has been described as large paper, is no different from the others; and whenever I have been able to trace the provenance, all copies, whether or not described as large paper, have coalesced into the single issue.

In his bibliography of the Bodoni Press in 1927, Mr. H. C. Brooks says that some copies were printed on *papier d'Annonay*. And at first glance this statement would seem to be supported by a copy sold at Hodgson's, 5 December 1930, lot 490, which was described (with a reference to Brooks) as printed on Annonay paper, boards, uncut.* I cannot assert with any conviction that no copies were printed on *papier d'Annonay,* for Bodoni's normal practice was to print some copies on a finer paper; but Miss Berry in November 1790 and De Lama in his bibliography of Bodoni in 1816 refer only to the copies on vellum as special copies, and all copies on paper that I have been able to examine are on the same good Italian laid paper. Only when the copy sold at Hodgson's in 1930 has been found can the uncertainty be resolved.

PLATES

The frontispiece and plates were prepared afterwards in London, but they are bound in with enough regularity to deserve description

* The phrase *papier d'Annonay* has at various times been used to apply both to any wove paper and to marbled paper, because both sorts were first made in France at the mills of Johannot and Montgolfier in Annonay; wove paper was first made in France in 1779. Bodoni used the phrase to mean wove paper made in Annonay.

Another possible source of confusion is the French tendency to describe any fine grade of wove paper as *papier vélin,* which in English translation can easily be confused with vellum. Finally, the bluish paper that Bodoni liked to use was first developed at Annonay. But it seems clear that De Lama in his bibliography of Bodoni lists copies on *papier d'Annonay* to mean wove paper manufactured at the mills in Annonay.

Longman's Catalogue of June 1813 may be taken to support the belief in a few copies on *papier d'Annonay:* a copy of the *Castle of Otranto,* 1791, is described as 'imperial octavo, russia, gilt, on fine vellum paper.' But I cannot trace that copy.

even if they are not properly part of the collation of the volume as prepared by Bodoni.

In March 1785 Reveley made a drawing of the castle of Otranto in Italy, and Lady Craven sent it to HW in November 1786. (Richard Bull inserted a water-color copy in his *Description of SH,* now WSL, and another smaller copy in his *Castle of Otranto,* now WSL.) The frontispiece was engraved from Reveley's drawing and printed, presumably in 1791 in London, on Whatman paper: it exists in three states, two or more of which are frequently found together in copies of the book.

A. Plain foreground, no clouds, no lettering.

B. Two figures in foreground, clouds, engraver's name (Barlow). This is actually a new plate, not merely state A with added detail.

C. Like state B, but with lettering below.

Six plates illustrative of the *Castle of Otranto* were published by E. and S. Harding in July 1793 to accompany either the Bodoni or the small octavo edition; they were drawn by 'a lady' (Miss Anne Melicent Clarke) and engraved by Birrell. The plates were of course not issued with any copies sold before July 1793, but a good many purchasers of the book after that date seem to have had the plates bound in. These engravings are better known from their use, with new lettering, in Sivrac's Italian translation in 1795, for which they are usually said to have been prepared; they were then issued again in Jeffery's editions of 1796 and 1800.

COPIES ON VELLUM

Although Miss Berry says that only five copies were printed on vellum, De Lama says specifically in his bibliography of Bodoni that six were printed on vellum, four of which were sent to London. At least four of these six can be traced.

1. The copy formerly owned by Marshal Junot, Duc d'Abrantes; citron morocco; listed in his *Catalogue,* lot 295. This copy has the original title-page, 'Printed with Bodoni's characters, 1790,' and the uncorrected text throughout. It was sold in the Junot Sale at Evans's in 1816 for £9.9.0; Sotheby's, 3 August 1867 (George Smith Sale), lot 7954; Sotheby's 12 April 1902 (E. G. Hibbert Sale), lot 882, to B. F. Stevens, £190; Anderson Galleries, 19 January 1912 (Hoe Sale, Part 2), lot 3419, $60; now in the Huntington Library.

2. Bound in blue morocco, with a drawing on title-page; without the frontispiece. Evans, 5 April 1815 (James Edwards Sale), lot 165, to the Duke of Devonshire, £29.8.0; in 1944 still in the library at Chatsworth.

BIBLIOGRAPHY OF HORACE WALPOLE

3. Bound in blue morocco, with the plates printed on satin. Offered for £16.16.0 in Edwards's Catalogue for 1794, lot 2306. Probably this was the George Galwey Mills copy sold by Jeffery, 24 February 1800, lot 181; and it may have been the same copy that was offered at Christie's, 25 April 1804, lot 254. But this copy seems to be unrecorded since 1804, unless it is copy 4.

4. Eton College (in the Storer Collection).

5. The Golowkin-Galitzin copy; lot 128 in the Galitzin Sale, 1825, 249 francs. It is recorded in the Supplement to the *Catalogue de la bibliothèque du roi . . . sur vélin*, 1828, p. 115; it is still presumed to be in the Bibliothèque Nationale.

COPIES ON PAPER

1. Inscribed by HW: 'Lord Orford begs Mrs. Dickenson's acceptance of this Parmesan Edn. of his *Castle of Otranto*, May 9th, 1792.' This copy had the original title-page, 'Printed with Bodoni's characters, 1790.' Mrs. Dickenson is undoubtedly Mrs. Mary (Hamilton) Dickenson, 1756–1816; one is tempted to think this copy may have been the uncorrected copy that HW read in December 1790. Bound in calf; Sotheby's, 9 April 1935 (Miscellaneous Sale), lot 350, to Maggs, £13.

2. HW's copy, with frontispiece in states A and B; final blank leaf wanting; four drawings by Bertie Greathead and two portraits inserted; also a letter by HW (in Kirgate's hand save for signature; the original was in the Waller Sale in 1921) and one by Edwards; bookplate of Lord Orford on half-title, of the Earl of Cromer and of Robert Hoe inside cover. Probably SH Sale, vii.76 (London Sale, 1030), to Payne and Foss, £1.11.6 (with the Italian translation of 1795); rebound for Lord Gosford in red morocco with his crest on sides, by C. Lewis. Puttick and Simpson, 1 May 1884 (Gosford Sale), lot 3071, to Harvey, £7; Christie's, 1 April 1897 (Reginald Cholmondeley Sale), lot 114, to Quaritch, £11.5.0; thence to John W. Ford, who owned this copy in 1905. Sotheby's, 21 May 1909 (Miscellaneous Sale), lot 362, to B. F. Stevens, £15.5.0; Anderson Galleries, 19 January 1912 (Hoe Sale, Part 2), lot 3420, $60; Sotheby's, 10 December 1913 (Library of an American Amateur, i.e., Hoe), lot 173, to Edwards, £7; thence apparently to the Earl of Cromer; Edwards, March 1937, to WSL, £20. A copy of the Bodoni edition in the Carysfort Library (Major R. G. Proby, Elton Hall, Peterborough) preserves copies of the Greathead drawings and a copy of HW's letter.

3. Bound in tree calf, rebacked with purple morocco; bookplates of Lord Aldenham and of E. V. Utterson; four watercolors by Wright; frontispiece in state C; preliminary blank leaf wanting. Sotheby's, 20 March 1857 (Utterson Sale), lot 1702, £2; Sotheby's, 24 May 1886 (Addington Sale), lot 627, to Ellis, £3.3.0. Listed in Lord Aldenham's Catalogue, 1888, p. 192; Sotheby's, 12 June 1933 (Aldenham Sale), lot 483, to Maggs, £4.4.0; Maggs, August 1933, to WSL, £8.8.0.

4. Contemporary red morocco, inscribed on fly-leaf: 'G. Birch, a present from the noble author, Horace Walpole, Earl of Orford, 1792,' and one correction in MS in the text of Birch's poem. This commendatory poem, published in *St.*

James's Chronicle of 20 June 1765, was first reprinted with the *Castle of Otranto* in this edition. Frontispiece in state C. Sold by Brentano's, October 1939, to WSL, $37.50.

5. Bound in white vellum, with Etruscan border on blue ground, attributed to Edwards of Halifax; frontispiece in states A and C; now at Yale.

6. Bound in vellum, gilt back, uncut; bookplates of the Earl of Orford of Mannington Hall and of Francis A. Gaskill. Sotheby's, 11 June 1895 (Orford Sale), lot 326, to Harvey, £2.8.0; re-offered in Orford Sale, 14 March 1902; offered in an English bookseller's catalogue (I have seen only a clipping, with no date or name) for 18/–; now at the Newberry Library.

7. Contemporary mosaic morocco, in the style of continental bindings of about 1730; frontispiece in state B. Dealers' labels of W. Robinson, Liverpool, and Menno Hertzberger, Amsterdam. International Antiquariaat, Amsterdam, April 1933, to WSL, 112.5 guilders. A copy in a similar binding, with the Birrell plates on India paper mounted on heavier paper and colored, was sold at the American Art Association in 1925; Maggs Brothers offered in 1931–34 what appears to have been the same copy. Mr. G. D. Hobson of Sotheby's, who has studied these bindings with care, suggests to me that such copies were prepared for the luxury trade on James Edwards's order; Mr. Hobson has records of a number of other books published by Edwards or his associates and similarly bound.

'A new edition. London: Printed in the year 1793.' Printed in 12mo. in half-sheets; the text has 200 pages.

'A new edition. London: Printed for Wenman and Hodgson, No. 144, Fleet-Street, 1793.' Printed in 18mo. in sixes; the text has 157 pages.

'Last edition adorned with cuts.' Berlin: Himbourg, 1794. Engraved title-page and four plates by J. W. Meil. Octavo; the text has 152 pages.

COPIES

1. Green morocco, gilt edges; the author's own copy, with engraving of his seal; illustrations by Meil. Sotheby's, 28 November 1883 (Beckford Sale, Part 3), lot 351, to Quaritch, £3.10.0.

2. Contemporary blue boards, with plates bound at end; bookstamp of Schlossbibliothek, Dessau. Edgar Wells, October 1931, to WSL, $7.50.

In 1794 the *Castle of Otranto* was reprinted, with large omissions, in *The New Wonderful Magazine, and Marvellous Chronicle* (Vol. 4), pp. 117–140.

Italian translation by George Sivrac, London, 1795. For this edition the six Harding plates of 1793, engraved by Birrell from drawings by Anne Melicent Clarke and often bound in copies of the Parma edition (see above), were relettered in Italian. The frontispiece was engraved by Thomas Medland from a drawing by Joino.

Signatures: Four leaves unsigned; b²; B–Q⁸; R⁷.

Pagination: [i] half-title; [ii] blank; [iii] title-page; [iv] blank; [v] Dedication to HW; [vi] blank; [vii]–x editor's preface; [xi] 'Indice'; [xii] blank; [1]–253 text; [254] errata.

Cancel: Leaf B₆, which seems to be a cancel in all copies, may have been printed as R₈.

States and Variants

On page viii a footnote has been added in many copies to identify the English editor of the Parma edition, Edwards; but the earlier state without the footnote is not rare. To make room for the footnote, one line was shifted to the bottom of page vii.

This edition was printed on three kinds of paper and on vellum, to produce four issues:

(1) on ordinary thin wove paper, watermarked clearly 1794 in block numerals.

(2) on *papier vélin*, a heavier, smooth-surfaced wove paper watermarked E & P [i.e., Edmeads and Pine].

(3) on *papier vélin* both larger and thicker, royal octavo, watermarked dimly 1794 in the corner of the sheet.

(4) on vellum.

Copies

1. Rebound in modern panelled calf, gilt, by Rivière; half-title wanting. Original sepia drawing by Joino for the frontispiece inserted. S. Baker of Paris, November 1937, to wsl, $27.

2. Contemporary mottled calf; on *papier vélin*. Name on fly-leaf: Anne Melicent Clarke. (Miss Clarke, from whose drawings the plates were made, was the daughter of Charles Clarke and Anne Radcliffe, and niece of Sir Charles Farnaby-Radcliffe, Bart. In 1802 she married E. H. Delmé.) Gift of Lewis Buddy, III, to wsl, November 1929.

3. Red morocco by Hering; on *papier vélin*. Pasted in is a slip with note by HW: 'Miss Clark, niece of Sir Charles Ratcliffe, made the drawings for the prints to the Castle of Otranto.' Bookplate of HW. SH Sale, vii.76 (London Sale, 1030), to Payne and Foss, £1.11.6; probably the copy offered by Payne and Foss, *Catalogue of Spanish and Italian Books*, 1845, lot 788, £2.2.0; offered for 18/– in a clipping from an unidentified catalogue; American Art–Anderson, 14 October 1931 (Miscellaneous Sale), lot 201, $12.

4. On large paper, contemporary tree calf, gilt; label of Kerr and Richardson, Glasgow. Plates bound together at end. Gift of Edward L. McAdam, Jr., to A. T. Hazen.

5. A copy printed on vellum is, or at least was, in the Bibliothèque Nationale. Either the same or another copy was sold for 79 francs in the MacCarthy Sale.

Jeffery's edition; octavo. Printed by Cooper and Graham, 1796. This edition includes the frontispiece and plates of Sivrac's edition; but they are so handsomely colored with ornamental borders that the lettering is obscured. The text is printed on Whatman wove paper watermarked 1794; leaves G_4 and G_5, the two inner leaves of the gathering, seem to be a cancel quarter-sheet.

STATES AND VARIANTS

All copies I have seen printed on paper are on the same paper; the title-page reads: 'Price one pound seven shillings in boards, with coloured plates and borders.' A few copies were printed on vellum, with the same statement of price on the title-page. It seems unlikely that copies on vellum were sold at that price.

In 1797 Jeffery reissued his edition with a cancel title-page; the plates are not colored. The title-page reads: 'Price half a guinea in boards.'

COPIES OF 1796 EDITION

1. Red morocco; note on fly-leaf by George Daniel: 'Beckford's copy, from the Fonthill Library.' Sotheby's, 27 July 1864 (Daniel Sale), lot 1727, to Rye, £2.5.0. Now WSL.

2. Blue morocco, with water-color flowers painted as borders to the plates by the Misses Berry. Sotheby's, 27 July 1864 (Daniel Sale), lot 1728, to Boone, £1.13.0; owned in 1936 by Mrs. Scott-Murray, Heckfield Place.

3. Printed on vellum. Copies are in the Bibliothèque Nationale (it cost 59 francs in the Galitzin Sale in 1825), British Museum, and John Rylands Library. A fourth vellum copy, bound in russia, with colored plates printed on satin, was sold at Christie's, 30 April 1917, for £2.15.0.

French translation: *Isabelle et Theodore; histoire traduite de l'anglais d'Horace Walpole.* Paris, Lepetit, 1797. Two volumes, 16mo.

Jeffery's second edition; octavo and quarto. Printed by Blackader, 1800. The octavo edition is printed on paper watermarked C & S 1798; the quarto is watermarked 1794; both issues are printed from the same type, with altered imposition. Although the collation of the octavo edition by signatures is the same as the edition of 1796, the type has all been reset. Although the plates do not have colored borders, the notice is kept on the title-page of the octavo, undoubtedly copied in error from the edition of 1796.

LATER EDITIONS

Cooke's pocket edition, 1800. There were various issues of this edition, both before and after 1800.

London, 1801; 12mo.

New York: The Shakespeare Gallery, 1801.

Harrison's edition, London, 1803; small octavo; issued in weekly parts.

London: Printed for T. Hughes by T. Plummer, 1804. An abridgment of 36 pp., 12mo.

London: Printed by J. Wright, for Vernor and Hood, 1804; 179 pp.; 16mo in half-sheets.

London, 1808; with Clara Reeve's *Old English Baron;* 16mo.

London: Printed by W. Wilson, for Vernor, Hood, and Sharpe, 1809; 196 pp.; 12mo.

In Vol. 22 of Mrs. Barbauld's 'British Novelists,' 1810; reprinted in 1820.

Edinburgh, Ballantyne, 1811; introduction by Sir Walter Scott; quarto. In a copy at Harvard the introduction has extensive revisions in Scott's hand.

London, 1811; with Clara Reeve's *Old English Baron;* 12mo.

London, A. K. Newman, 1815.

London, Thomas Kelly, 1817. Also issued in Kelly's 'Select Novels.'

In Ballantyne's 'Novelists Library'; octavo; 1823.

London, Hurst, 1823; in *Novels of Sterne* [etc.]

C. Whittingham, Chiswick Press, for T. Tegg [etc.]; 1823; 16mo.

London, J. Limbird, 1824; in Limbird's 'British Novelist.' Re-issued in 1825.

London, Baynes and Son, 1825; with *Old English Baron.* Other editions published with the *Old English Baron* are dated by the British Museum [1830?] and [1840?].

London, Jones and Co., 1825; 'University edition.'

London, Bentley, 1834; with *Vathek* and *The Bravo of Venice.* Re-issued in 1836.

Hartford, Conn., published serially in *The Scrap Book,* 1835–6.

In Farmington there is a series of playbills for Covent Garden, December 1840 to February 1841, when a Christmas pantomime called *The Castle of Otranto* was performed nearly fifty times. Also at Farmington is a somewhat earlier playbill for 'A grand romantic extravaganza, founded on *The Castle of Otranto.*'

London, Joseph Thomas, 1840. With memoir of the author by G. M. B.

Philadelphia, 1840.

In 'Clarke's Home Library,' [1844].

In Bohn's *Classic Tales*, with nine other novels; 1852. Re-issued in 1860 and in 1882.

Philadelphia, 1854.

London, Ward and Lock, 1856; in one volume with Lewis's *Bravo of Venice*.

Edinburgh, 1858.

London, [1872]; with *Old English Baron*. These two novels were variously issued without date both in London and New York.

London, J. C. Nimmo and Bain, 1883; with *Old English Baron*.

London, 1886; edited by Henry Morley, in Cassell's 'National Library.' Re-issued in New York and in Leipzig.

New York, 1886; in Munro's 'Seaside Library.'

New York, J. B. Alden, 1889.

London, 1906; in 'The York Library'; re-issued in 1923.

London, Chatto and Windus, 1907; with Scott's Memoir and a Preface by Caroline F. E. Spurgeon, in 'The King's Classics.' Re-issued many times in London, Boston, and New York; in 1907, 1923, [1925?], 1926, 1929, 1930.

London, Constable, 1924; with *Mysterious Mother*; edited by Montague Summers. Reproductions of the plates from Jeffery's edition of 1796, and a useful but not wholly accurate bibliography of the early editions of *The Castle of Otranto*.

London, Scholartis Press, 1929; edited with an introductory essay by Oswald Doughty.

In numerous recent textbook anthologies of short novels: Everyman's Library, 1930; Scribner's, 1931; Kronenberger's *Eighteenth Century Miscellany*, 1936; Beaty's *Short Novel*, 1940.

A new translation into French by Dominique Corticchiato was published by his father, José Corti, at Dijon in 1943. The translator was only seventeen when he completed his work in 1941; he was sent to a labor camp during the German occupation and was not seen again.

18. ACCOUNT OF THE GIANTS. 1766.

'Short Notes': '28, 29 June 1766. Wrote an *Account of the Giants lately discovered*. It was published 25 August following.'

HW to Cole, 1 February 1768: 'I have sent you no Patagonians, for they are out of print, I have only my own copy and could not get another. Pray tell me how or what you heard of it, and tell me sincerely, for I did not know it had made any noise.' Cole's reply, 16 February 1768, names two friends who have praised the little book to him. The *Gentleman's Magazine* reviewed it in September 1766.

Small octavo in half-sheets; published 25 August by Noble, at 1/–;
approximately 19 x 12.3 cm. uncut.
Signatures: Two leaves unsigned; B–E⁴.

AN

ACCOUNT

OF THE

GIANTS

LATELY DISCOVERED;

In a Letter to a Friend in the Country.

LONDON:

Printed for F. NOBLE, opposite *Gray's-Inn,*
Holborn.

MDCCLXVI.

Pagination: Half-title, with copyright notice on verso; title-page with verso blank; 1–31 text, signed at end 'S. T.' and dated 1 July 1766; [32] blank.

EDITIONS

There seems to have been only a single edition of the little satire, perhaps because of the bookseller's lack of enterprise. HW included it in the SH edition of his *Works* in 1770, and in the *Works* of 1798. It was reprinted in the first volume of *The Repository* in 1883.

A translation into French by the Chevalier de Redmond, in MS, was in the SH Sale, vi.123, to Edwin Keats, Esq., and is now in the Bodleian.

COPIES

1. HW's copy, with his autograph and MS notes. Offered by T. Thorpe, *General Catalogue*, Part 4 (1844), item 8595.
2. HW's copy, untrimmed, in his *Collection of Tracts of George III*, Volume 15, now WSL. The collection is recorded in the *SH Bibliography*, p. 255.

The *Account of the Giants* is a somewhat scarce book, but there are two other copies at Farmington, three at Harvard, one at Yale, and one in the Library of Congress. Other copies in the United States are recorded at the Boston Public Library, John Carter Brown Library, the Hispanic Society in New York, and the Huntington Library.

19. HISTORIC DOUBTS ON . . . RICHARD III. 1768.

HW to Cole, 19 December 1767: 'My *Richard III* will go to the press this week, and you shall have one of the first copies, which I think will be in about a month. . . . Mr. Gray went to Cambridge yesterday sennight; I wait for some papers from him for my purpose.'

HW to Lord Hailes, 17 January 1768: 'I will beg to know how I may convey my *Richard* to you, which will be published to-morrow fortnight. I do not wonder you could not guess the discovery I have made. It is one of the most marvellous that ever was made. In short, it is the original Coronation Roll of Richard the Third, by which it appears that very magnificent robes were ordered for Edward the Fifth, and that he did, or was to have walked at his uncle's coronation. This most valuable monument is in the great Wardrobe. It is not, though the most extraordinary, the only thing that will surprise you in my work.'

The principal printed source was Sir George Buck's *History of Richard III*, in folio, 1646. In his 'Epistle from Florence' in 1740, HW had called Richard 'the assassin king,' but in 1767 Buck's defense of Richard was a congenial textbook. In his eager advocacy of Richard, HW was a better apologist than historian; his belief (pp. 114–16) that Shakespeare's *Winter's Tale* is filled with refer-

HISTORIC DOUBTS

ON THE

LIFE AND REIGN

OF

King RICHARD the Third.

By Mr. HORACE WALPOLE.

L'Histoire n'est fondée que sur le temoignage des Auteurs qui nous l'ont transmise. Il importe donc extremement, pour le sçavoir, de bien connoitre quels etoient ces Auteurs. Rien n'est à negliger en ce point; le tems où ils ont vecû, leur naissance, leur patrie, la part qu'ils ont eue aux affaires, les moyens par lesquels ils ont été instruits, et l'intérêt qu'ils y pouvoient prendre, sont des circonstances essentielles qu'il n'est pas permis d'ignorer: delà depend le plus ou le moins d'autorité qu'ils doivent avoir: et sans cette connoissance, on courra risque très souvent de prendre pour guide un Historien de mauvaise foi, ou du moins, mal informé.

Hist. de l'Acad. des Inscript. Vol. X.

LONDON:

Printed for J. DODSLEY in Pall-Mall.
M.DCC.LXVIII.

19.

ences to Anne Boleyn and Henry VIII will perhaps suggest how his mind worked. But what he wrote he wrote well.

In Lord Derby's library at Knowsley there is a copy that HW seems to have used for a working copy; bound in are many extracts he had made from original records, and other materials. Signature P is a proof-sheet, with MS corrections that were incorporated in the first edition. On the title-page HW has written: 'Begun to be printed 23 December; finished 27 January.' On p. 120 he has noted two misprints of the second edition (only one was corrected in 1770), and has jotted down an item that he used in a note in 1770. From the proof of Signature P it is possible to understand a minor error in a reference on p. 113 of the first edition: the note came at the bottom of p. 112, but HW made an insertion that forced the printer to move three lines to the next page, and the footnote was not corrected.

'Short Notes': '1 February 1768. Published my *Historic Doubts on Richard the Third*. I had begun it in the winter of 1767; continued it in the summer, and finished it after my return from Paris. Twelve hundred copies were printed, and sold so very fast that a new edition was undertaken the next day of 1,000 more, and published the next week.'

HW to Cole, 1 February 1768: 'I have waited for the impression of my *Richard*, to send you the whole parcel [of books] together.'

HW to Lord Hailes, 2 February 1768: 'I have sent to Mr. Cadell my *Historic Doubts*, Sir, for you. . . . I can attribute to nothing but the curiosity of the subject, the great demand for it; for though it was sold publicly but yesterday, and twelve hundred and fifty copies [in his 'Short Notes' he wrote twelve hundred] were printed, Dodsley has been with me this morning to tell me he must prepare another edition directly.' Dodsley had paid £100 for the copyright, and so was doubtless as much pleased as HW by the book's success.

'Short Notes': '20 June. Received a letter from Voltaire desiring my *Historic Doubts*. I sent them.' Mme. du Deffand, who had been corresponding with HW about the book for many months, received her copies on March 1st.

Quarto; published 1 February 1768 by James Dodsley, at 5/–.
Signatures: a–b⁴; B–S⁴.
Pagination: [i] title-page; [ii] blank; [iii]–xv Preface, dated 28 November 1767; [xvi] blank; 1–134 text; [135] Addition; [136] Errata and directions to binder.
Two plates: a frontispiece (King Richard), and a picture of the King and Queen facing p. 103. The original drawing by Vertue for the second plate was in the SH Sale, xi.112, and is now WSL.

STATES AND VARIANTS

It is clear from HW's correspondence with Gray that he had difficulty with the passage (pp. 116 ff.) about Jane Shore. I think from the watermarks that the whole of Signature Q was reprinted or else delayed by a final revision; but Dodsley used three lots of paper somewhat indiscriminately, so that one cannot be certain.

EDITIONS

The second edition, printed quickly and published 12 February, 1768, is a page-for-page (almost line-for-line) reprint, with errata corrected. Corrections on pp. 132 and 135 were not followed in the *Works* of 1770 and 1798, the text of which must have been printed from the first edition. The second edition is printed on the paper used for the last sheet and preliminaries of the first edition. It is all reset, including the Preface, except for some scattered pages in the last few sheets: apparently the type had been only partly distributed when Dodsley decided to reprint.

The Dublin edition of 1768, printed for Faulkner and others, is in duodecimo, 166 pages.

A French translation, published in 1800 in octavo by Lerouge and Debray, is said in the preface to have been translated by Louis XVI about 1782 and revised in the Tuileries.

A new edition published in London in 1822, in octavo, is a reprint of the first edition; the Errata are copied without being adapted to the new pagination.

ADDITIONS AND REPLIES

Gibbon wrote a long review of *Historic Doubts* in *Mémoires littéraires de la Grande Bretagne pour l'an 1768*, published in May 1769. To this review some observations by David Hume were appended as notes. (See 'Short Notes,' 1769.) HW was more disturbed by Hume's objections than by any others: see his letter to Cole, 16 April 1768, long before Hume's notes had been published. It was particularly as a reply to Hume (but also to the *Critical Review* and to a series of letters in the *London Chronicle*) that HW wrote his *Supplement to the Historic Doubts*, printed in the quarto *Works* in 1771, the second volume, but published only in 1798. In 1860 Edward Craven Hawtrey published the text in the sixth volume of the Philobiblon Society. Miss Berry had sold HW's MS to White of Pall-Mall, from whom Hawtrey bought it; later he presented it to Eton College. The first ninety-six pages of Hawtrey's text agree with the text in the *Works;* the next four pages are omitted in the *Works;* the rest of the text is the same.

The first separately printed answer to *Historic Doubts* was by F. W.

Guidickens, *An Answer to Mr. Horace Walpole's Late Work*, 99 pages, published by White in May 1768.

In the first volume of *Archaeologia*, 1770, Dean Jeremiah Milles published his 'Observations on the Wardrobe Account.'

In January 1771 Robert Masters read *Some Remarks on Mr. Walpole's Historic Doubts* before the Society of Antiquaries. They were printed as an offprint from *Archaeologia* by Richard Gough, and thirty copies were given to Masters about 24 December 1772 to distribute as presents; published in the second volume of *Archaeologia* in April 1773. When Cole offered to try to find a copy of the twenty-page offprint, HW replied that he was not in any eagerness to see a copy. (See HW to Cole, 8 January 1773; to Mason, 9 January 1773; to Cole, 7 April 1773.)

HW wrote his reply to Dean Milles in August 1770, and to Masters early in 1774; in the *SH Bibliography,* pp. 89 and 95, I suggested that HW printed both replies together, in the quarto *Works,* in 1774. But a letter from Michael Tyson, 1 February 1772 (printed in Nichols's *Lit. Anec.,* viii.579) asserts that HW has printed the *Reply to Dean Milles* and that Cole has a copy; and soon after Gray's death, Mason wrote to HW, 28 August 1771: 'I have in my possession [i.e., among Gray's papers] your printed letter to Dr. Milles.' It was therefore a printed copy that HW asked Gray to show to Cole in January 1771.

HW left his last word on Richard III in a short *Postscript to the Historic Doubts,* written in 1793 and printed by Miss Berry in the *Works,* 1798.

COPIES

1. HW's copy, contemporary calf, gilt; with prints and drawings (including the naked Jane Shore); HW's bookplate and MS notes. SH Sale, iv.142, to Bohn, £3.10.0; Sotheby's, 3 July 1883 (Beckford Sale, Part 3), lot 254, to Lord Rosebery through Bain, £50. (B. W. Currie wanted it, but Quaritch did not want to bid above £50 for him, according to Quaritch's letter now at Farmington.)

2. HW's copy, described as Large Paper, but actually a part of the 1770 *Works* in royal quarto; contemporary calf; HW's bookplate and MS notes (including the Postscript written in 1793). SH Sale, vii.33 (London Sale in June, viii.1049), to Holloway of Henrietta Street. Owned by Edward Herries (1821?–1911); sold by David C. Herries to Hodgson; Hodgson, September 1942, to WSL, £31.10.0. The book contains some dozen MS notes, chiefly identifications; since most of them were not used in 1798, it is likely that Miss Berry printed from another copy. The text of the Postscript is the same as that printed in 1798, but the punctuation differs; Kirgate's transcript of the Postscript was in the Waller Collection.

3. A copy with HW's bookplate is in the Dyce Collection at the Victoria and Albert Museum.

4. William Cole's copy, with copious MS notes; sent to Cole 1 February 1768. On the fly-leaf is a copy of a letter from HW to George Steevens, December 1782, disparaging Cole. T. King, 20 May 1800 (Steevens Sale), lot 1149, to Baker, £3.5.0; Sotheby's, 8 June 1825 (Baker Sale), lot 831, to Corrie, £1.3.0; Evans, 18 June 1846 (Upcott Sale), lot 1094, to Burn, £1.13.0; Puttick and Simpson, 24 June 1875 (Robert Lee Sale), lot 194, to Hayes, £2.3.0.

5. Michael Lort's copy, with his name on fly-leaf; MS notes and newspaper clippings; the answer by Guidickens bound in at end; nineteenth-century calf. Sotheby's, 20 April 1791 (Lort Sale), lot 3711, 11/–; Boone, 1862, to H. H. Gibbs, later Lord Aldenham, 36/–; Sotheby's, 5 May 1937 (Aldenham Sale), lot 1045, to Maggs for WSL, £2.2.0 (with Nicholl's *Wills*).

6. Lord Dacre's copy, with his bookplate; MS notes on end-papers; contemporary calf. Sotheby's, 7 November 1938 (Barrett-Lennard Sale), lot 34, to Maggs for WSL, £1.10.0.

7. The Duke of Richmond's copy, probably presented by HW; red morocco, with Richmond crest on spine. Gift of Mr. Philip Hofer to WSL, December 1933.

8. Presentation copy to David Dalrymple, Lord Hailes, inscribed by him; contemporary calf. Sotheby's, 25 May 1937 (Newhailes Sale), lot 423, to Elkin Mathews, £5.10.0; Elkin Mathews, July 1937, to WSL, £6.1.0.

9. Gibbon's copy with his first bookplate; contemporary calf, rebacked; in Gibbon Sale, 1832. Note on fly-leaf: 'This volume was purchased at the sale of Gibbon's library at Lausanne in 183 , by Mr. Broomfield, and presented to me in 1833. The library, purchased by Beckford after Gibbon's death, was disposed of by auction at that time. J. D.' (See Keynes's *Catalogue* of Gibbon's library.) Goodspeed, May 1940, to WSL, $10.

10. Sir John Fenn's copy, with his bookplate and autograph; a few corrections in MS; bound in calf with other tracts in 1774. The set is recorded in *SH Bibliography*, p. 67.

11. Presentation copy to Lord Harcourt: now at Nuneham Park.

12. Presentation copy to George Onslow, sent with a covering letter 31 January 1768, when Onslow's father, the former Speaker of the House, was near death; a sketch of HW by H. E. Onslow, made after HW's death, tipped in; old calf. Sotheby's, 14 July 1902 (Miscellaneous Sale), to Maggs, £3.5.0; Anderson Galleries, 26 March 1912 (Allis Sale), lot 877, $35; now in the Huntington Library.

13. A copy described as a presentation copy, with several added portraits, red morocco. Sotheby's, 15 February 1871 (Corser Sale), lot 595.

14. Presentation copy, calf, with a bookplate initialled: Gmo. P. D. D. H. W. This may very possibly have been William Parsons. Sotheby's, 28 April 1894 (Buckley Sale), lot 4229.

20. THE MYSTERIOUS MOTHER. 1768.

For description see the *SH Bibliography*, pp. 79–85. Copy 8 on p. 84 should be listed as the edition of 1781: it was presented to William Parsons in 1790, and is now owned by William Zimmerman, Jr. Mr. Zimmerman also owns Horace Mann's copy of the edition of 1768.

21. WORKS. 1770; *and* REPLY TO DEAN MILLES.

For description see the *SH Bibliography*, pp. 87–96. I now think, chiefly on the evidence of a letter from Tyson to Gough, 1 February 1772, printed in Nichols's *Literary Anecdotes* viii.579, that the *Reply to Dean Milles* was printed soon after it was written, in 1770. See also under *Historic Doubts*, 1768, above.

22. DESCRIPTION OF STRAWBERRY-HILL, &c. 1774.

For description see the *SH Bibliography*, pp. 105–112.

23. LETTER TO THE EDITOR OF . . . CHATTERTON. 1779.

For description see the *SH Bibliography*, p. 116.

24. DESCRIPTION OF STRAWBERRY-HILL. 1784.

For description see the *SH Bibliography*, p. 123.

25. ESSAY ON MODERN GARDENING. 1785.

First printed in the fourth volume of the *Anecdotes of Painting*. For description see the *SH Bibliography*, p. 129. Considerable extracts were included in the new edition (1801) of *Observations on Modern Gardening* by Thomas Whately (*d*. 1772).

26. HIEROGLYPHIC TALES. 1785.

For description see the *SH Bibliography*, pp. 133–4. Thomas Barrett's copy, listed as Copy 5, was purchased by WSL at the Hartshorne Sale, 3 November 1945, for $135.

27. THE WORKS IN QUARTO. FIVE VOLUMES, 1798.

Although the nominal editor of the *Works* was Robert Berry, his daughter, Mary Berry, did the work. She made a careful collection of HW's published and unpublished writings, making use of the partially completed *Works* of 1770, and carrying out the directions left in manuscript by HW. The result is a handsome and satisfying memorial to the literary life of her dear friend. She omitted numerous ephemeral pieces, it is true, but these five volumes supplemented by HW's letters and his historical memoirs present a relatively complete picture.

According to C. H. Timperley's *Dictionary of Printers and Printing*, 1839, p. 797, the copyright of the *Works* 'is said to have produced £3000.'

THE
WORKS
OF
HORATIO WALPOLE,
EARL OF ORFORD.

IN FIVE VOLUMES.

VOL. I.

LONDON:

PRINTED FOR G. G. AND J. ROBINSON, PATERNOSTER-ROW,
AND J. EDWARDS, PALL-MALL.

MDCCXCVIII.

27. FIRST ISSUE. REDUCED. WIDTH OF ORIGINAL 14.8 cm.

THE
WORKS
OF
HORATIO WALPOLE,
EARL OF ORFORD.

IN FIVE VOLUMES.

VOL. I.

LONDON:

PRINTED FOR G. G. AND J. ROBINSON, PATERNOSTER-ROW,
AND J. EDWARDS, PALL-MALL.

MDCCXCVIII.

27. SECOND ISSUE. REDUCED. WIDTH OF ORIGINAL 14.1 CM.

The first two volumes are a line-for-line reprint of the unpublished *Works* of 1770. Miss Berry was thus able to use the sheets of that edition for some copies, especially the *Catalogue of Royal and Noble Authors,* pp. 1–520, in the first volume.

Royal quarto, on wove paper with various watermarks; approximately 31.5 x 24.8 cm. uncut. Large-paper copies are on laid paper, imperial quarto; a good trimmed copy at Farmington measures 35 x 28 cm.

Volume I. *Signatures:* Two leaves unsigned; a–b⁴; c²; B–4C⁴; 4D²; 4E³; one leaf, printed with sheet 4E, is inserted after 4A₃.

Pagination: [i] half-title; [ii] blank; [iii] title-page; [iv] blank; [v]–xx Preface by the Editor; xxi HW's Advertisement; [xxii] blank; [xxiii]–xxiv Contents; 1–567 *Fugitive Pieces* and *Royal and Noble Authors;* [568] blank; [569]–577 Indexes; [578] blank; one leaf, 549*–550*, inserted after p. 550.

The preliminary leaves of all five volumes were printed last, as usual. The three pages of Directions to the Binder, often missing, may appear after half-sheet c in the first volume, with which they seem to have been printed, or at the end of the fifth volume: these Directions list the plates in the five volumes.

Leaf a₂ (in the Preface) is a cancel; I do not know why, but I suppose Miss Berry made some change in her comments. Perhaps she inserted the reference to the Postscript to the *Historic Doubts,* which is itself a cancel in the second volume.

Volume II. *Signatures:* Two leaves unsigned; a¹; B–Ee⁴; Ff²; *Ff–*Ii⁴; two leaves unsigned; Gg–4D⁴.

Pagination: Half-title, title-page, and Contents, with versos blank; [1]–220, [*221]–*252, [221]–576 *Castle of Otranto, Historic Doubts, Aedes Walpolianae, Description of the Villa, On Modern Gardening,* etc.

Half-sheet Ff² and the half-sheet before Sig. Gg are *not* parts of the same sheet; the compositor copied the pagination of the SH *Works* of 1770 but altered the imposition.

Leaf *Ii₄ (the Postscript to *Historic Doubts,* pp. *251–2) is a cancel, watermarked 1797 like the preliminary leaves of all five volumes. This Postscript was written in 1793, and was perhaps overlooked at first by Miss Berry. HW's manuscript, from which Miss Berry presumably took her text, is inserted in his annotated copy of *Historic Doubts* (actually, sheets from SH *Works* of 1770), now WSL. A copy of the Postscript in Kirgate's hand was in Sir Wathen Waller's collection.

Volume III. *Signatures:* Two leaves unsigned; a²; B–3T⁴.
   Pagination: Half-title and title-page, with versos blank; [v]–vii Contents; [viii] blank; [1]–512 *Anecdotes of Painting* and Indexes.
Volume IV. *Signatures:* Two leaves unsigned; a²; B–3N⁴; 3O².
   Pagination: Half-title and title-page, with versos blank; [v]–vii Contents; [viii] blank; [1]–463 *Catalogue of Engravers* and miscellaneous pieces; [464] blank; [465]–468 Indexes to *Engravers*.
Volume V. *Signatures:* Two leaves unsigned; a¹; B–4Q⁴; 4R².
   Pagination: Half-title and title-page, with versos blank; [v]–vi Contents; [1]–675 Letters; [676] blank.

PLATES

The Directions to the Binder list 165 plates; one other, Lord Herbert (i.230), seems to have been omitted by inadvertence. The position of the plates may vary somewhat, but since the plates have page numbers for this edition, they can readily be identified. The frontispiece to the first volume is a portrait of HW drawn by Thomas Lawrence in 1796; according to Lord Glenbervie's *Diary*, the frontispiece was prepared as early as September 1797. The other plates in the first four volumes are new impressions of plates previously used by HW; the portraits of HW's correspondents, in the fifth volume, were engraved for this edition by James Heath.

The first volume has engravings of coins on pp. 155 and 321; the fourth volume has engravings on pp. 377 and 380. The five title-pages have respectively the third SH fleuron, the first fleuron, the second fleuron, the fleuron from the SH edition of *Anecdotes*, and a new fleuron drawn by Heath.

At Farmington there is a collection of the plates, clearly extracted from several sets of the *Works*, containing several copies of each plate.

STATES AND VARIANTS

When this edition was published in June, 1798, it was priced at £10.10.0 in boards (£21 for sets on large paper). For five sumptuous volumes with 166 plates, the price was perhaps not exorbitant; but sales seem to have been slow and the edition remained in print for a good many years. During these years, it is clear that new impressions of the plates were prepared from time to time, as needed. In what may be called the original impression, the plates are on paper watermarked 1794 or 1795. But I have seen a set in which the plates are on paper watermarked 1804, another set watermarked 1805, a third set watermarked 1807, and a fourth set watermarked variously from 1806 to 1812. Five issues of the plates can be differentiated, therefore, by the watermarks; others may exist. The plates were reissued (without the *Works*) by Jeffery on Whatman paper watermarked 1822, and partial sets of this issue often occur in extra-illustrated volumes prepared by Walpolian or SH collectors; it was one such set that I recorded in the *SH Bibliography*, p. 108.

A new set of title-pages (and half-titles) was printed about 1805. The paper is watermarked 1805, and the plates of this issue (in five sets examined) are watermarked either 1805 or 1807. The reprinted title-pages can be identified most easily by the watermark, since the watermark in all title-pages of the first issue is 1797; furthermore, the pointed 'A' in the fourth line, 'Horatio Walpole,' is readily identifiable in contrast to the characteristic blunt Caslon 'A' of the first issue. The set at the University of Illinois is in original boards, with paper labels.

A third issue of the *Works* can also be dated approximately by the watermarks, about 1812. One set at Farmington (a similar set is at the University of Illinois) has title-pages of the first issue, but the plates are watermarked variously from 1806 to 1812; this set is in original boards, uncut, with printed paper labels reading: 'The Works of Horatio Walpole, Earl of Orford. 176 [i.e., 166] plates. In five volumes. . . . Price £15.15.' This increased price for the remainder of a work published at ten guineas in 1798 is an interesting illustration of the effects of the sudden inflation during the war, 1810–1815.

One other variant, recorded in *SH Bibliography*, p. 93, can properly be repeated here. Some sheets of the SH *Works* of 1770 were incorporated in some copies of the published edition. I have seen three sets (two at Farmington and one at the University of Illinois) in which pp. 1–520 of the first volume consist of sheets from the SH *Works* of 1770; in a copy at the Metropolitan Museum in New York, pp. 9–520 are from the SH *Works*. In another copy at Farmington, sheet M of the second volume is from the SH *Works;* and Mr. W. Rees-Mogg of Bristol, England, writes that in his copy sheet D of the first volume and sheet N of the second are from the SH *Works.* No doubt unidentified fragments from the SH *Works* lurk in still other copies of the published edition of 1798.

GERMAN TRANSLATION

A collection of miscellaneous pieces (*On Modern Gardening, Reminiscences, Hieroglyphic Tales,* and other pieces from the fourth volume), translated into German by A. W. Schlegel, was published at Leipzig in 1800.

CONTENTS

It may be of interest to record the pieces that were first published in 1798, indicating by a parenthetical 1770 those that HW had printed in the SH *Works* of 1770. Numerous corrections, especially in the text of the *Fugitive Pieces,* were prepared by HW when he planned the edition of his *Works.*

i.xxi HW's Advertisement.

i.452 Additions to *Royal and Noble Authors* (1770).

i.526 Pieces omitted.

i.562 Appendix to *Royal and Noble Authors.*

ii.185 Supplement to *Historic Doubts* (1770).

ii.251* Postscript to *Historic Doubts.*

ii.289 *Nature Will Prevail:* written in 1773, printed probably soon afterwards in 1770 *Works,* produced in June 1778 at the Little Theatre in the Haymarket.

ii.305 *Thoughts on Tragedy and on Comedy:* written in 1775-6, after the success of Jephson's *Braganza,* for which HW furnished an Epilogue.

ii.323 Detection of a late forgery called *Testament politique du Chevalier Robert Walpoole.*

'Short Notes': '1 February 1767. Began the detection of the *Testament Politique* of my father at Strawberry Hill; and finished it the next time I went thither, February 17th. Did not print it, as no translation was made into English of that fictitious work.' In the *Works* it is dated 16 February.

ii.339 *Life of Rev. Thomas Baker* (1656–1740), Cambridge antiquary. Written in 1778 from William Cole's materials.

HW to Cole, 22 September 1777: 'I return you your MS. . . . It has amused me much, and I admire Mr. Baker for having been able to show so much sense on so dry a subject. I wish, as you say you have materials for it, that you would write his life. . . . PS. . . . If you are busy yourself, and will send me the materials, I will draw up the life of Mr. Baker.'

Cole to HW, 4 October 1777: 'Nothing could please me more than your proposal in the PS. The materials I have, I am afraid will be scanty.' 7 October 1777: 'I am extremely busy in collecting my materials about Mr. Baker. . . .'

HW to Cole, 15 October 1777: 'Pray do not hurry yourself about the anecdotes of Mr. Baker. . . . I shall certainly not have time to do anything this year. I . . . shall probably have not much idle leisure before next summer.'

Cole to HW, 29 March 1778: 'I finished my collections relating to Mr. Baker, which are ready to be sent to you whenever you are disposed to have them.'

HW to Cole, 23 April 1778: 'Your Bakeriana will be very welcome about June.' 10 June 1778: 'You shall send me your papers whenever you please. . . . I shall write the life to oblige you, without any thoughts of publication, unless I am better pleased than I expect to be, and even then, not in my own life. I had rather show that I am sensible of my own defects, and that I have acquired judgment enough not to hope praise for my writings; for surely when they are not obnoxious, and one only leaves them behind one, it is a mark that one is not very vain of them.'

Cole to HW, 4 July 1778: 'Mr. Lort . . . returns to town on Tuesday, and engages to deliver my packet into your own hands.'

HW to Cole, 24 July 1778: 'I have commenced the life, and do not dislike my ideas for it, if the execution does but answer.' 1 September 1778: 'I have resumed Mr. Baker's Life, and pretty well arranged my plan, but I shall have little time to make any progress till October.' 26 October 1778: 'I have finished the Life of Mr. Baker, will have it transcribed, and send it to you. . . . I have no thoughts of printing this Life at present; nay, I beg you will not only not communicate it, but take care it never should be printed without my consent. . . . I have executed it by snatches and with long interruptions.' 3 January 1779: 'I have made my printer, now my secretary, copy out the rest of Mr. Baker's Life.' 15 January 1779: 'I send you . . . my Life of Mr. Baker. . . . I beg you will communicate my MS to nobody—but if you think it worth your trouble, I will consent to your transcribing it. . . . I shall beg to have it returned to me . . . for I have nothing but the foul copy.'

Cole's transcript is now in the British Museum.

ii.363 *Account of my Conduct,* written in 1782, with Letters to and from Ministers.

HW's preliminary sketch and notes are now WSL. The completed MS, dated 30 March 1782, is now in the British Museum among the Berry papers.

iv.234 *Additional papers relative to Chatterton.*

These papers are a supplement to his *Letter to Chatterton,* printed at SH in 1779. The MS in the Morgan Library contains a few additional paragraphs that HW evidently intended to be printed in the *Works.*

BOOKS BY WALPOLE

iv.247 *Narrative of the Quarrel between Hume and Rousseau,* written in September 1767.

The Letter to Rousseau with which HW stirred the quarrel was printed in the *St. James's Chronicle* in 1766.

iv.271 *Reminiscences,* written in 1788.

HW wrote these Reminiscences for Mary and Agnes Berry. Two MSS are now in the Morgan Library. Since their first printing in the *Works* they have been reprinted as follows:

1805. A beautiful edition, limited to 25 copies, printed by Richard Taylor and Co. for Lord Frederick Campbell. (See J. Martin, *Bibliographical Catalogue,* 1834, p. 100.)

1818. Printed for John Sharpe.

1819. Reprinted, with Letters of HW, etc. (Another edition was published in 1819 in Sharpe's Select Edition of the British Prose Writers.)

1820. A Boston reprint of Sharpe's edition.

1830. In Whittingham's Cabinet Library.

1840. In the first volume of Bentley's edition of HW's *Letters.*

1857. In the first volume of Cunningham's edition of HW's *Letters.*

1924. Edited by Dr. Paget Toynbee, for the Clarendon Press; printed with the *Reminiscences* in this edition are HW's *Conversations with Lady Suffolk,* from HW's *Book of Materials* now in the Folger Library.

In 1826 a French translation was published at Paris.

iv.355 Parody of Lord Chesterfield's *Letters,* 1774.

'Short Notes': 'May 1774. Wrote an introduction to, and a parody of, Lord Chesterfield's three first Letters.' See HW to Lady Ossory, 11 August 1774: 'Mr. Cambridge came yesterday and said he must ask to see something I had lately written. . . . He . . . meant the parody of Lord Chesterfield's *Letters.* . . .' The MS is now in the Morgan Library.

iv.361 *Criticism on Johnson.* The MS is now in the British Museum.

iv.363 *Continuation of Baker's Chronicle:* dated 28 December 1782.

iv.368 *Detached Thoughts.*

The MS is now in the Morgan Library. The text was reprinted from the *Works* by Lewis Buddy in 1905.

iv.371 Miscellaneous Verses. These are all reprinted and annotated by wsl in his edition of *HW's Fugitive Verses,* 1931; I add bibliographical notes on a few poems.

'The Funeral of the Lioness,' written in 1751. HW's MS, from the Waller Collection, is now in the Merritt Collection at Harvard; HW's transcript is in the *Waldegrave MS,* now wsl. The texts are nearly the same.

'Verses on Celia,' 1750.

'The Parish Register of Twickenham.' HW's MS, now wsl, shows that the first, rejected title was 'The Inmates of Twickenham.' In 1784 (the MS in the 'Book of Visitors' is dated 7 September 1784) he added a postscript of ten lines, in honor of Lady Diana Beauclerk who had moved to Twickenham. In HW's copy of *Description of SH* 1774, now WSL, is a copy of the revised poem, with extensive notes, all in HW's hand. The text printed in 1798 has three verbal alterations.

'Countess Temple appointed Poet Laureate to the King of the Fairies.'

'Portrait of Mme. du Deffand,' 1766.

'Lines to Lady Anne Fitzpatrick,' September 1772.

'Epitaph on Lady Ossory's Bullfinches,' *ca.* 1779.

'Card to Lady Blandford,' 15 August 1778.

'The Advice, 1763.'

Song: 'What a rout do you make.'

'To Love' from Petrarch.

'To Lady Craven,' 1778.

iv.396 Prologue and Epilogue to *Mysterious Mother*.

iv.402 Epilogue to *The Times*, 1779. The text published with the play is very different. See under the year 1780 in the second part, below.

iv.403 Epigram on the New Archbishop of Canterbury, 1758.

iv.404 Epigram on the translation of Anacreon.

Epigram: 'When Theseus from the fair.' HW's transcript is in the 'Book of Visitors' (see *Correspondence with Mary and Agnes Berry*, 1944, ii.269).

Three riddles.

iv.407 'Epitaphium vivi auctoris,' 1792.

iv.409 Letters to and from Richard West.

The fifth volume is entirely made up of letters to various correspondents.

ADDITIONAL VOLUMES

Pendant to the five volumes of 1798 are the following, all in quarto:

Volume VI. *Letters . . . to George Montagu*. London, Rodwell and Martin, and Henry Colburn, 1818. And *Letters . . . to the Rev. William Cole*, printed later in 1818 for the same publishers. A few copies were printed on large paper. These two volumes may be bound together, or either one may appear separately, with an added title-page: The Works . . . Vol. VI. London, Rodwell and Martin, and Edinburgh, Blackwood, 1818.

With the *Memoires* of 1822, Murray issued for this volume an added title-page: The Works . . . Vol. VI. London, John Murray, 1822.

See further under *Letters*, 1818.

Volumes VII, VIII. *Memoires . . . of George the Second*. London, John Murray,

1822. Two volumes. These two volumes were also issued with added title-pages: The Works . . . Vol. VII [VIII]. London, John Murray, 1822.
See also under *Memoires*, 1822.

Volume IX. *Letters . . . to the Earl of Hertford. . . . To which are added Mr. Walpole's Letters to the Rev. Henry Zouch*. London, Charles Knight, 1825. This volume was also issued with an added title-page: The Works . . . Vol. IX. London, Charles Knight, 1825.
See also under *Letters*, 1825.

COPIES OF WORKS 1798

1. Presentation copy from Mary Berry to Hannah More (1745–1833), with letter from Miss Berry dated 19 May 1798 and Hannah More's signature. Later inscription by Hannah More: 'For J. S. Harford, Esqr., my much esteemed friend, Blaise Castle. Barley Wood.' Bookplate of John S. Harford, Jr. (1785–1866). Half-calf, 5 volumes; Directions to Binder at end of fifth volume. Sotheby's, 11 December 1930 (Miscellaneous Sale), lot 1101, to Maggs for WSL, 20/–.

2. Mrs. Piozzi's copy, with her marginal notes in *Letters to Montagu*. Bookplate of George Folliott. Title-pages and plates on paper watermarked 1805; pp. 1–520 of first volume from SH *Works*. Half-calf, 7 volumes (Letters to Montagu and to Cole bound separately). Sotheby's, 12 May 1930 (Miscellaneous Sale), lot 131, to WSL, £9.10.0.

3. Large-paper copies seem to be quite uncommon, but there are undoubtedly some sets in country house libraries. The copy at Farmington, handsomely bound in contemporary red morocco, came from Elkin Mathews, September 1927, for £14.14.0. Another fine set is at Harvard.

28. NOTES TO THE PORTRAITS AT WOBURN ABBEY. 1800.

HW to Lady Ossory, 30 September 1791: 'I have been ashamed to write to your Ladyship till I could tell you that I have finished the notes to the Duke of Bedford's pictures; I stayed at home all yesterday evening to make an end; but alas! Madam, though I have been so tedious, if your partiality for me has raised any expectation of amusement in the Duke, his Grace will be piteously disappointed; of which I warned your Ladyship before I undertook the task, in the execution of which I have no kind of merit but obedience. . . . Well, I said I had done my work, and now I will have it transcribed fair and transmit it to your Ladyship; but you must not expect it incontinently, for poor Kirgate is shaking in bed with an ague and fever, and nobody else can read my sketches.'

HW to Lady Ossory, 26 October 1791: 'Your Ladyship is very gracious about the catalogue, as I knew you would be, when you had commanded it. . . .' 23 November 1791: 'The Duke of Bedford is too gracious, Madam, in being pleased to say he is content with my meagre account of his pictures. . . .'

NOTES
TO THE
PORTRAITS
AT
WOBURN ABBEY.
28.

Kirgate's fair copy of the MS is now at Woburn Abbey. It is apparently the copy in SH Sale, vi.150, and then in the Eyton collection: the heading 'By Horace Earl of Orford' must be later than 5 December 1791, when HW succeeded as fourth Earl; and HW's description of his handwriting in his letter to Lady Ossory, 30 September (quoted above), does not suggest the 'neat autograph' described in the Eyton catalogue. What was described as the original MS, 'in the neat autograph of the author,' 14 pp., small quarto, was sold at Sotheby's, 22 May 1848 (Eyton Sale), lot 1484, to Lilly, 17/–. Eyton's copy of the printed booklet may well be the copy now at Farmington.*

The booklet was not printed until 1800. A correspondent who signed himself 'C.D.' sent HW's notes to the *European Magazine,* saying they had been omitted from the *Works* but had been printed privately; the *European Magazine* printed them in January and February, 1801, and they were also printed in the *Annual Register* for 1801. Many extracts from HW's notes were printed in 1825 by Henry Bone in his *Catalogue of Miniature Portraits at Woburn Abbey.* Some extracts from HW's notes were also included in *A Descriptive Catalogue of the Portraits in the Collection of John, Duke of Bedford, K.G., at Woburn Abbey,* of which fifty copies were printed privately in 1834.

Large quarto; approximately 31 x 25 cm. untrimmed, on laid paper. (A copy at Farmington on wove paper has been trimmed to the size of a post quarto.)

Two sheets, the second signed B.

Pagination: [1] 'Notes to the Portraits at Woburn Abbey'; [2] blank; [3]–16 text.

STATES AND VARIANTS

The copy in the British Museum and the copy sold with Mrs. Damer's books, unlike the copy reproduced here, have the date on the title-page.

29. LETTERS . . . TO GEORGE MONTAGU. 1818.

The editor of the *Letters* was John Martin, the bibliographical bookseller. The book was advertised in the *Morning Chronicle,* 2 April 1818. The trade edition, in royal quarto, was offered at two guineas in boards; a few copies were printed on imperial paper and priced at three guineas each.

The editor deleted many of the personal names in the text of the

* The record of HW's earlier visit to Woburn Abbey, in 1751, is in *Visits to Country Seats* (in the sixteenth volume of the Walpole Society), and in his letter to Montagu, 8 October 1751.

LETTERS

FROM THE

HON. HORACE WALPOLE,

TO

GEORGE MONTAGU, ESQ.

FROM THE YEAR 1736, TO THE YEAR 1770.

NOW FIRST PUBLISHED FROM THE ORIGINALS,

IN THE POSSESSION OF THE EDITOR.

LONDON:
PRINTED FOR RODWELL AND MARTIN, NEW BOND STREET,
AND HENRY COLBURN, CONDUIT STREET.
1818.

29. REDUCED. WIDTH OF ORIGINAL 13.5 cm.

Letters. Some time after the publication of the volume, an eight-page supplement, 'Names of Persons mentioned in the Foregoing Letters,' was circulated privately, according to the reviewer in the *Quarterly Review*. Perhaps the circulation was not sharply restricted, because bound copies of the *Letters* are likely to have the supplement at the end, and the sequence of signatures indicates that the printer prepared the supplement to be so placed.

This collection of letters, often bound with the *Letters to Cole,* was also issued with an added title-page as Vol. VI of the *Works, 1818,* published by Rodwell and Martin of London, and Blackwood of Edinburgh. With the *Memoires* in 1822, Murray also issued a new title-page for Vol. VI, to be used by purchasers who wanted to make a set.

A second edition of the *Letters to Montagu,* in quarto, with most of the names inserted in the text, was printed in 1819. Copies are in the British Museum, Bodleian, University of Edinburgh, and the State College of Washington.

Some unsold copies of the second edition seem to have been reissued in 1834 with a new title-page, the imprint of which reads: London, Published for Henry Colburn by R. Bentley; Bell and Bradfute, Edinburgh; and John Cumming, Dublin. Two copies with this title-page are in the Forster Collection at the Victoria and Albert Museum.

A French translation of the *Letters to Montagu* was published at Paris in 1818.

30. LETTERS . . . TO THE REV. WILLIAM COLE. 1818.

The same John Martin who edited the *Letters to Montagu* from the MSS owned by Lord Frederick Montagu was presumably the editor of this volume. The Preface is dated December 1818. The trade edition was printed in royal quarto, to match the *Works* of 1798 and the *Letters to Montagu;* a few copies were printed on imperial paper.

Copies bound with the *Letters to Montagu* were issued as Vol. VI of the *Works,* with added title-page, and again in 1822, as described above under *Letters to Montagu.*

A reissue described on the title-page as a second edition was published in 1824; the imprint reads: London, Printed for Henry Colburn, New Burlington-Street, and Rodwell and Martin, Bond-Street.

LETTERS

FROM THE

HON. HORACE WALPOLE,

TO THE

REV. WILLIAM COLE,

AND OTHERS;

FROM THE YEAR 1745, TO THE YEAR 1782.

NOW

FIRST PUBLISHED FROM THE ORIGINALS.

LONDON:

PRINTED FOR RODWELL AND MARTIN, BOND STREET,

AND

HENRY COLBURN, CONDUIT STREET.

1818.

30. REDUCED. WIDTH OF ORIGINAL 13.4 CM.

BOOKS BY WALPOLE

Two copies with this title-page are in the Forster Collection at the Victoria and Albert Museum.

31. LETTERS . . . TO THE EARL OF HERTFORD. 1825.

The editor of this quarto volume, published by Charles Knight, was John Wilson Croker. It was likewise issued, with added title-page, as Vol. IX of the *Works*, the *Memoires* of 1822 being counted as Volumes VII and VIII. It was published 12 July 1825 (*Morning Chronicle*), at £1.11.6, in royal quarto; no copies on large paper are mentioned in the advertisement, and presumably none were printed.

COLLECTED EDITIONS OF THE LETTERS

Miss Berry published the first collection of HW's letters in the *Works* in 1798; many letters are included in the second, fourth, and fifth volumes. They are recorded in this bibliography only in the contents of the *Works*. Occasional letters have been first published in many places, for example, in the *Literary Correspondence of John Pinkerton* in 1830; but since such items will be recorded in the appropriate volume of the Yale edition, they are omitted here.

The principal collected editions of HW's letters are the following:

Private Correspondence of Horace Walpole, Earl of Orford. Now first collected. London: Rodwell and Martin, and Colburn and Co. 1820. Four volumes, 8vo.

Correspondence with George Montagu [etc.] Printed for Henry Colburn, 1837. Three volumes, 8vo. A new edition of the *Private Correspondence*.

Letters to Sir Horace Mann, edited by Lord Dover, 1833. Three volumes, 8vo.; second edition, 1833. Completed in *Letters to Sir Horace Mann . . . Concluding Series*, 1843-4. Four volumes, 8vo. The first series was reprinted in New York, 1833, in two volumes, 8vo.; the concluding series was reprinted in Philadelphia, 1844, in two volumes, 8vo.

The Letters of Horace Walpole, Earl of Orford. London, Richard Bentley, 1840. Six volumes, 8vo. The letters to Mary and Agnes Berry, first printed in this edition, are in the sixth volume. The editor was John Wright. Reprinted in Philadelphia in 1842, and in London in 1846.

Letters addressed to the Countess of Ossory, edited by R. Vernon Smith, 1848. Two volumes, 8vo. Second edition, 1848. Reprinted without notes, 1903, in three volumes.

Correspondence of Horace Walpole and William Mason, edited by John Mitford, 1851. Two volumes, 8vo.

LETTERS

FROM THE

HON.BLE HORACE WALPOLE,

TO

THE EARL OF HERTFORD,

DURING HIS LORDSHIP'S EMBASSY IN PARIS.

TO WHICH ARE ADDED

Mr. WALPOLE'S LETTERS TO THE Rev. HENRY ZOUCH.

———

LONDON:

PRINTED FOR CHARLES KNIGHT, PALL-MALL-EAST.
———
MDCCCXXV.

31. REDUCED. WIDTH OF ORIGINAL 13.3 cm.

Letters, edited by P. Cunningham, 1857. Nine volumes, 8vo. Many times reprinted in London and New York.

Some unpublished letters of Horace Walpole, edited by Sir Spencer Walpole, 1902. One volume, 8vo.

Letters, edited by Mrs. Paget Toynbee, Oxford, 1903–5. Sixteen volumes, 8vo. Supplementary volumes edited by Paget Toynbee, 1918–25. Three volumes, 8vo.

The Correspondence of Gray, Walpole, West, and Ashton, edited by Paget Toynbee, Oxford, 1915. Two volumes, 8vo.

The Yale Edition of Horace Walpole's Correspondence, edited by W. S. Lewis, New Haven, 1937–.

Closely related series of letters, both of which include extracts from HW's letters, are:

Letters of the Marquise du Deffand to the Hon. Horace Walpole, ed. by Mary Berry, 4 vols., 1810. Many editions down to Mrs. Toynbee's, in 3 vols., in 1912.

Extracts from the Journals and Correspondence of Miss Berry, ed. by Lady Theresa Lewis, 3 vols., 1865.

32. MEMOIRS OF THE REIGNS OF GEORGE II AND GEORGE III. 1822–59.

These historical memoirs, perhaps HW's most important work, were published in three installments: *The Memoires of the last ten years of George II,* 1822; *Memoirs of . . . George III,* 1845; and *Journal of . . . George III from 1771 to 1783,* 1859. The MSS from which they were printed fill twenty-one small folio volumes, in Lord Waldegrave's collection. Drafts of several passages are at Farmington, and numerous fragmentary notes. Also at Farmington are the MSS of the memoirs for 1783–91, still unpublished; they were acquired by Richard Bentley from Mary Berry, and were sold to WSL in 1937 by the present Mrs. Bentley.

The importance HW attached to his *Memoirs* may be judged from the frontispiece Bentley drew for him. (See the edition of 1822.) He wrote and rewrote them with great care, and his final copy of the earlier part was carefully prepared for the printer, with head- and tail-pieces by Bentley and Müntz pasted at the proper places. The frontispiece was perhaps designed in 1752, although some of the other drawings seem to have been made as late as 1758 or 1759.

'Short Notes': 'About this time [1751] I began to write my *Memoirs*. At first, I intended only to write the history of one year.'

HW to Montagu, 6 June 1752: 'The memoirs of last year are quite finished, but I shall add some pages of notes, that will not want anecdotes.'

'Short Notes': '28 October [1759], I finished the eighth book of my *Memoirs*. . . . 10 October 1763, began the *Memoirs* of 1759; 28 October, finished that year; 29 October, began the year 1760; 9 November, finished that year. . . .

MEMOIRES

OF THE

LAST TEN YEARS

OF THE

REIGN OF GEORGE THE SECOND.

BY

HORACE WALPOLE, EARL OF ORFORD.

FROM THE ORIGINAL MSS.

IN TWO VOLUMES.

VOL. I.

LONDON:
JOHN MURRAY, ALBEMARLE-STREET.
MDCCCXXII.

32. REDUCED. WIDTH OF ORIGINAL 13.8 cm.

18 August 1766. Began *Memoirs of the Reign of George the Third*. . . . In July and August [1769] finished two more books of my *Memoirs,* for the years 1765, 1766. . . . 18 October 1769, began another book of the *Memoirs;* 1 December 1769, finished the *Memoirs* to the end of the first Parliament of George III. . . . 1771. This year wrote the *Memoirs* of 1768, 1769, 1770. 7 January 1772, began the *Memoirs* of 1771; 20 April 1772, finished my *Memoirs,* which conclude with the year 1771; intending for the future only to carry on a Journal.'

In the MS the *Memoirs* of 1754-55 are marked 'Begun 26 December 1755'; those of 1756 'Begun 8 August 1758'; those of 1757 'Begun 9 October 1758'; those of 1758 'Begun 17 August 1759'; those of 1759 '10 October 1763'; and those of 1760 '29 October 1763.'

The Parallel of Sir Robert Walpole and Mr. Pelham, which is included under the year 1751 in the printed *Memoirs,* was written in 1747. HW marked his transcript in the *Waldegrave MS:* 'inserted . . . with some slight alterations' in the *Memoirs.*

PUBLICATION

The different sections of these *Memoirs* or historical journals were published as follows:

1. *Memoires of the last ten years of the reign of George the Second,* 1822. Two volumes, royal quarto, published 4 March 1822 at five guineas in boards (*Morning Chronicle*). The editor was Lord Holland. These two volumes were also issued as the seventh and eighth volumes of the *Works* of 1798-1825; the last sheet of the second volume contains title-pages for Vols. VI (Letters to Montagu and Cole, 1818), VII, and VIII.

Copies are occasionally described as on large paper, but since the advertisement says nothing about such copies and since I have never been able to find any, I think none were printed.

A new edition was published in 1846, in three volumes, octavo; reprinted in 1847; some extracts were published in the second volume of *Classic Memoirs* (New York 1901). Translated into French, in two volumes, in 1823. A German translation of the *Memoirs* of George II and George III was published in 1846-7.

2. *Memoirs of . . . George III,* 1845. Four volumes, octavo, edited by Sir Denis Le Marchant; reprinted in 1851 and again (re-edited by G. F. R. Barker) in 1894. A reprint was published by Lea and Blanchard in Philadelphia in 1845.

3. *Journal of . . . George III from 1771 to 1783,* 1859. Two volumes, octavo, edited by Dr. Doran. Reprinted in 1910 as *Last Journals of Horace Walpole.*

MEMOIRS

OF THE REIGN OF

KING GEORGE THE THIRD.

By HORACE WALPOLE,

YOUNGEST SON OF SIR ROBERT WALPOLE, EARL OF ORFORD.

NOW FIRST PUBLISHED FROM THE ORIGINAL MSS.
EDITED, WITH NOTES,
By Sir DENIS LE MARCHANT, Bart.

VOL. I.

LONDON:
RICHARD BENTLEY, NEW BURLINGTON STREET,
Publisher in Ordinary to Her Majesty.
1845.

32.

JOURNAL OF THE REIGN

OF

KING GEORGE THE THIRD,

FROM THE YEAR 1771 TO 1783.

BY HORACE WALPOLE.

NOW FIRST PUBLISHED FROM THE ORIGINAL MSS.

"For 'tis a chronicle of day by day."—SHAKSPEARE, *Tempest*.

"On prévoioit que la patrie allait être sacrifiée à la dignité de la famille royale, dont la véritable gloire est de se sacrifier toujours au bonheur de la patrie."—VIE DE MAINTENON, tom. v., page 18.

EDITED, WITH NOTES, BY DR. DORAN,
AUTHOR OF 'HISTORY OF THE QUEENS OF ENGLAND OF THE HOUSE OF HANOVER,' ETC.

IN TWO VOLUMES.—VOL. I.

LONDON:
RICHARD BENTLEY,
Publisher in Ordinary to Her Majesty.
M.DCCC.LIX.

The right of Translation is reserved.

32.

33. NOTES ON LORD CHESTERFIELD'S WORKS. 1867.

These notes were communicated to the Philobiblon Society by R. S. Turner. The pamphlet was issued separately, and also in the *Miscellanies of the Philobiblon Society*, Vol. XI. An earlier and less correct edition had been printed in the tenth volume.

HW's copy (SH Sale, vii.40; i.e., London Sale 1056) is now in the British Museum.

34. NOTES ON THE POEMS OF ALEXANDER POPE. 1871.

These notes were edited by Sir William A. Fraser, Bt., from HW's set of Pope's *Works*, 1742–51, then in his possession, and printed in 1871 in an edition of fifty copies. In 1876 a more complete text was reprinted in an edition of 300 copies. HW's set is now wsl. In the *Huntington Library Quarterly* for July 1938, George Sherburn reprinted HW's annotations in *Additions to the Works of Alexander Pope* (2 vols. 1776), from HW's copy now in the Huntington Library.

35. JOURNAL OF THE PRINTING OFFICE. 1923.

Dr. Paget Toynbee printed this *Journal* of HW's private press, from the MS formerly owned by Sir Wathen A. Waller, Bt. At the Waller Sale in 1921 the MS was sold to Abdy (Sir Robert Abdy?) for £90; Maggs Bros., June 1933, to wsl, £150.

The American issue of the *Journal* includes important facsimiles of items in the collection of E. P. Merritt now at Harvard.

36. STRAWBERRY HILL ACCOUNTS. 1927.

In 1927 Dr. Paget Toynbee printed this valuable record, published by the Clarendon Press, from the original MS owned by Colonel Alan F. Maclure of Manchester.

37. MISCELLANEOUS ANTIQUITIES, EDITED BY W. S. LEWIS. 1927–40.

In 1772 HW printed two volumes of *Miscellaneous Antiquities* and then dropped the project, both from boredom and from lack of material. In 1927 Mr. Lewis began to publish Walpolian oddments, chiefly from MSS in his own collection. The complete list is detailed at the end of the sixteenth volume, published in 1940. I record herewith the brief titles of all that are strictly Walpolian:

III. *A Commonplace Book of Horace Walpole's*, 1927.

V. *Horace Walpole's Fugitive Verses*, 1931. This volume gathers, from the *Letters* and elsewhere, HW's occasional verses. It is referred to throughout this bibliography as *HW's Fugitive Verses*. Since its publication many unpublished verses have come to light.

HORACE WALPOLE'S MARGINAL NOTES,

WRITTEN IN DR. MATY'S MISCELLANEOUS WORKS AND MEMOIRS OF THE EARL OF CHESTERFIELD.

2 vols. 4to. 1777.

COMMUNICATED BY R. S. TURNER, ESQ.

The poffeffor of the volumes.

NOTES ON THE POEMS OF

ALEXANDER POPE,

BY HORATIO EARL OF ORFORD.

CONTRIBUTED BY

SIR WILLIAM AUGUSTUS FRASER,

OF LEDECLUNE AND MORAR, BARONET,

M.A., F.S.A.

FROM THE COPY IN HIS POSSESSION.

LONDON:
PRINTED AT THE CHISWICK PRESS.
1871
34.

VI. *The Forlorn Printer . . . Thomas Kirgate,* 1931.
VII. *Anecdotes Told Me by Lady Denbigh,* 1932.
VIII. *Horace Walpole's Letter from Madame de Sévigné,* 1933.
XI. *The Duchess of Portland's Museum,* 1936.
XII. *Bentley's Designs for Walpole's Fugitive Pieces,* 1936.
XIII. *Memoranda Walpoliana,* 1937.
XVI. *Notes by Horace Walpole on Several Characters of Shakespeare,* 1940.

38. SELECT OBSERVATIONS. 1937.

These extracts from HW's third *Book of Materials,* 1786, were printed at the Bibliographical Press in New Haven, 1937; one sheet in quarto. The MS is at the Folger Library.

BOOKS WITH EDITORIAL CONTRIBUTIONS BY WALPOLE

BOOKS
WITH EDITORIAL CONTRIBUTIONS
BY WALPOLE

39. GRATULATIO ACADEMIAE CANTABRIGIENSIS. 1736.

This handsome volume, printed at the University Press, was a semi-official publication of the University in honor of the marriage of the Prince of Wales. It includes verses in various languages, predominantly Latin, by University dignitaries, alumni, and students. Ashton and Gray, as well as HW, wrote in Latin; Gray's friend, Thomas Wharton, in Greek.

'Short Notes': 'In 1736 I wrote a copy of Latin verses, published in the *Gratulatio Acad. Cantab.*, on the marriage of Frederic, Prince of Wales.' The verses, entitled simply 'Ad Principissam,' were printed on the verso of leaf O_1; they were reprinted in 1931, in *HW's Fugitive Verses*, p. 99.

Prince Frederick and Princess Augusta were married 27 April 1736. The Cambridge volume was published late in May, and sold (according to the *Gentleman's Magazine*) by John Crownfield.

HW to Montagu, 20 May 1736: 'The verses are not published yet.'

It must have been printed by 24 May 1736 when West wrote to Gray, from Oxford: 'Your Hymeneal I was told was the best in the Cambridge Collection before I saw it, and indeed, it is no great compliment to tell you I thought it so when I had seen it, but sincerely it pleased me best.'

HW to Montagu, 30 May 1736: 'I shall send you soon . . . some poetry interspersed with prose: I mean the Cambridge Congratulation with the notes, as you desired.'

Folio; 38 leaves, without pagination; approximately 37.7 x 24.2 cm. trimmed.
Signatures: *²; B–T².

There are copies of the Cambridge *Gratulatio* in the British Mu-

GRATULATIO

ACADEMIAE CANTABRIGIENSIS

AUSPICATISSIMAS

FREDERICI

WALLIAE PRINCIPIS

ET

AUGUSTAE

PRINCIPISSAE SAXO-GOTHAE

NUPTIAS

CELEBRANTIS.

CANTABRIGIAE TYPIS ACADEMICIS.
MDCCXXXVI.

seum and Bodleian, and there are undoubtedly several copies in Cambridge libraries. A copy is at the University of Michigan, in a volume of pamphlets. The copy at Farmington, in contemporary boards covered with red silk, was sold by Spurr and Swift, August 1931, to WSL, £2.2.0. Also at Farmington, in one of Mitford's collections, is a single leaf (Q$_1$) containing Gray's verses.

HW's copy with MS notes, bound with the companion volume published at Oxford, is now in the Dyce Collection at the Victoria and Albert Museum. Dyce bought it at the SH Sale in 1842.

40. NARRATIVE OF THE LAST ILLNESS OF LORD ORFORD. 1745.

Although John Ranby's *Narrative,* with its implication that Dr. Jurin's powerful Lithontriptic Lixivium had contributed to Lord Orford's decay, produced a short but violent pamphlet war (a dozen pamphlets published between April and September) among medical men, I do not think it has ever been listed in a Walpolian bibliography. But on pages 15 to 32 a journal of Lord Orford's case from 3 February to 17 February 1745 is introduced with this statement: 'The ensuing Journal was kept with all imaginable exactness by one of his own sons, as well as by myself [i.e., Ranby].' I see no reason to doubt the truth of the statement. For one thing Ranby is always referred to in the third person in the journal, whereas he uses the first person elsewhere in his *Narrative.*

It would have been possible for one of the older sons, Robert or Edward, to keep such a journal, but it does not appear that they stayed at Arlington Street during their father's last illness; both were living elsewhere at the time, although they called to see their father more than once. But Horace was living at Arlington Street and he stayed close to his father all through February, being much moved by his father's suffering and much concerned about the medicines used. The regular notation on the progress of the case is entirely in Horace's manner, and is not characteristic of his elder brothers.

In an *Appendix,* published later as a rejoinder to one of his attackers, Ranby says on page 5 that everything he printed had been confirmed 'by the present Earl, and the greatest part of the family,' perhaps intending to differentiate from a later passage on page 35 where he repeats that the journal was 'kept by one of my Lord's sons.'

HW to Mann, 14 January 1745: 'My father has been extremely ill this week with his disorder; I think the physicians are more and more persuaded that it is the stone in his bladder. He is taking a preparation of Mrs. Stephens's medicine, a receipt of one Dr. Jurin, which we began to fear was too violent for him: I made his doctor angry with me by arguing on this medicine, which I never could comprehend. It is of so great violence, that it is to split a stone when it arrives at it, and yet is to do no damage to all the tender intestines through which it must

A
NARRATIVE
OF THE
LAST ILLNESS
OF THE
RIGHT HONOURABLE
THE
EARL of ORFORD:

From *May* 1744, to the Day of his Decease, *March* the Eighteenth following.

By JOHN RANBY,
Principal SERJEANT SURGEON to His
MAJESTY, and *F. R. S.*

LONDON:
Printed for JOHN and PAUL KNAPTON, in
Ludgate Street. M.DCC.XLV.
(Price One Shilling.)

40.

first pass. . . .' Years later, in annotating the poems of Sir C. H. Williams, HW asserted categorically that his father had been 'killed by Jurin's medicine' (*Works of Sir C. H. Williams,* 1822, i.206). He said the same thing in a note to his *Memoirs* for 1751.

HW to Mann, 28 February 1745. 'I have been out but twice since my father fell into this illness, which is now near a month; and all that time either continually in his room, or obliged to see multitudes of people. . . .'

It seems extremely likely to me that the journal printed by Ranby was written by HW, and that the book therefore deserves to be in a Walpolian bibliography. Perhaps the chief objection to including it is the presence of two copies in HW's library, with no comments whatsoever in either one.

Octavo in half-sheets; published 10 April 1745; approximately 21.3 x 13.5 cm. uncut.

Signatures: [A]–G⁴.

Pagination: [i] half-title; [ii] blank; [iii] title-page; [iv] blank; [v–viii] Preface; 1–47 text; [48] advertisements. One folded plate facing page 1.

STATES AND VARIANTS

Copies on large paper, royal octavo, lack the price at the bottom of the title-page. These were perhaps especially for the author's own use; one of HW's copies is on large paper.

In some copies, 'of' in the first line on page 6 is misprinted 'fo.'

A portrait of Lord Orford engraved by Proud, probably copied from another engraving, is inserted as a frontispiece in one copy. Although this may have been published by the Knaptons, it was not originally issued with Ranby's *Narrative*.

OTHER EDITIONS

The second edition with an *Appendix,* the latter sold separately to those who wanted it, was published in August.

COPIES

1. HW's copy, bound with Ranby's *Appendix,* ten other pamphlets on Ranby's *Narrative,* and two related tracts. Original half-calf, with HW's bookplate. SH Sale, iii.69, to Buckingham Palace Library (with other lots comprising in all 102 volumes of tracts), £86.12.6; the collection was sold through Quaritch, *ca.* 1920, to Sir Leicester Harmsworth; the trustees of Sir Leicester Harmsworth's estate sold these volumes (now 88), together with HW's *Tracts of George III,* through Quaritch to WSL in 1938.

2. HW's copy, on large paper, bound with *An authentick copy of the last Will and Testament of . . . R[obert] E[ar]l of O[rford]*. Old calf; bookplate of C. G. Milnes Gaskell. Probably SH Sale, vi.66, to Thorpe, £2 (with two other volumes); Hodgson's, 28 February 1924 (Milnes Gaskell Sale); Spurr and Swift, April 1926, to WSL.

3. William Cole's copy, in a volume of ten tracts, rebound in the nineteenth century and marked 'Miscellanies.' Bookplate of Lord Rosebery. Offered by B. White, 1784 (Cole's library), lot 8785, for 3/–; Sotheby's, 29 June 1933 (Rosebery Sale), in a collection of miscellaneous volumes; Stonehill, July 1933, to WSL, $12.

41. GRAY'S ELEGY. 1751.

A complete study of the *Elegy*, its composition and editions, belongs in a bibliography of Gray; but because HW arranged the publication with Dodsley, supplied the MS, and (presumably) wrote or edited the brief Advertisement prefixed to the poem in the early editions, the first edition belongs in a Walpolian bibliography.* The three extant MSS of the poem were printed in type and edited in 1933 by R. Fukuhara and H. Bergen; the poem's date has been brilliantly discussed by Mr. Garrod in *Essays presented to D. N. Smith*, 1945.

Gray to HW, 11 February 1751: 'Yesterday I had the misfortune of receiving a letter from certain gentlemen (as their bookseller expresses it) who have taken the *Magazine of Magazines* into their hands. They tell me that an *ingenious* poem, called, *Reflections* in a Country-Churchyard, has been communicated to them, which they are printing forthwith. . . . I have but one bad way left to escape the honour they would inflict upon me, and therefore am obliged to desire you would make Dodsley print it immediately (which may be done in less than a week's time) from your copy, but without my name, in what form is most convenient for him, but in his best paper and character. He must correct the press himself, and print it without any interval between the stanzas . . . and the title must be: Elegy, wrote in a Country Church-yard. If he would add a line or two to say it came into his hands by accident, I should like it better. . . . If Dodsley don't do this immediately, he may as well let it alone.'

Dodsley and HW worked to such good effect that the first edition was published 15 February, one day before the unauthorized edition in the *Magazine of Magazines*.

Gray to HW, 20 February 1751: 'You have indeed conducted with great decency my little *misfortune*. . . . Nurse Dodsley has given it a pinch or two in the cradle [misprints], that (I doubt) it will bear the marks of as long as it lives.

* It is likely that HW negotiated with Dodsley about publishing the *Eton Ode* (30 May 1747), inasmuch as Gray wrote to HW in June 1747 of 'your kind offices' as if they had just been exerted in his behalf. But the poem as published has no ascertainable Walpolian contribution.

Gray gave Dodsley the copyright for all his poems except the SH *Odes,* for which Dodsley paid him £40.

AN
ELEGY

WROTE IN A

Country Church Yard.

LONDON:
Printed for R. Dodsley in *Pall-mall*;
And sold by M. Cooper in *Pater-noster-Row.* 1751.
[Price Six-pence.]

But no matter... it will only look the more careless and by *accident* as it were. I thank you for your advertisement, which saves my honour.' In a later letter, 3 March 1751, Gray records four errors. One of these ('hidden' for 'kindred') was corrected in the second edition; the others were corrected in the third edition, which also introduces several other changes.

Quarto; approximately 27.8 x 22 cm. uncut; published 15 February 1751, at sixpence.
Signatures: [A]⁴; B².
Pagination: [1] title-page; [2] blank; [3] HW's Advertisement; [4] blank; [5]–11 text; [12] blank.

STATES AND VARIANTS

Much nonsense has been written concerning the 'first issue' of the first edition, with the reading 'hidden Spirit' instead of 'kindred Spirit.' But I cannot find that the first edition ever has the reading 'kindred.'

The first three editions were in fact printed from standing type: for the second edition the title-page was reset and 'hidden' corrected; for the third edition a dozen other corrections were made in the text, presumably in response to a letter from Gray. (The page numbers were reset in the second edition.) In other words, the *Elegy* went through three 'impressions,' with corrections, but since each new 'impression' received an edition number on the title-page, it is simpler to refer to 'editions.' Within the first edition, although catalogues like to boast that in a particular copy the word 'Finis' has punched through the paper or that the letter 'r' in the catchword on page 9 is in perfect alignment, I do not know that any significant indications of priority of issue exist.

The editions can be dated from the newspaper advertisements as follows: 1st edition, 15 February; 2d edition, 25 February; 3d edition, 14 March; 4th edition (1st setting), not until 7 April; 4th edition (presumably the 2d setting), 11 May.

The fourth (both settings) and later editions, though in the same format, were entirely reset. Mr. F. G. Stokes, in his exhaustive bibliography of the *Elegy* (1929), records the textual history of the poem during Gray's lifetime. In Robinson's Catalogue 59 (1936) what was described as Gray's copy of Dodsley's *Collection of Poems*, 1758, was offered; in the text of the *Elegy* Gray had made some corrections in MS.

EDITORIAL CONTRIBUTIONS BY WALPOLE

COPIES

Somewhat strangely, I have found no records of copies with any important contemporary association. (A presentation copy of the sixth edition 'From the Author' was offered at Sotheby's in 1927.) I do not doubt that Gray and HW owned copies, but I have no record of them. Yet even without association value, the *Elegy* has maintained a consistently high price, not because of extreme rarity but because it is so highly regarded. In the last twenty-five years one or two copies have been sold at auction each year, seldom bringing less than $1000, and any well-described copy brings several thousand dollars; the highest price on record seems to be in the Kern Sale in January 1929, $12,100. No other eighteenth-century printed volume that has survived in such numbers is in this class, save possibly the Kilmarnock Burns.

42. BENTLEY'S DESIGNS FOR SIX POEMS BY GRAY. 1753.

'Short Notes': 'This year [1753] I published a fine edition of six poems of Mr. T. Gray, with prints from designs of Mr. R. Bentley.' The four-page Explanation of the Prints was by HW himself.

Gray's hesitancy about publication and his nervous particularity about the text are fully documented in his *Correspondence*. There is a good summary in Straus's *Dodsley*, 1910, and also in Mr. R. Fukuhara's careful monograph in Japanese, Tokyo 1933. I quote only enough extracts to set forth the progress of the publication.

HW to Montagu, 13 June 1751: 'Our charming Mr. Bentley . . . is drawing vignettes for his [Gray's] Odes; what a valuable MS I shall have!'

Gray to HW, 8 September 1751: 'I send you this ["Hymn to Adversity"] (as you desire) merely to make up half a dozen, though it will hardly answer your end in furnishing out either a head or tail-piece.'

HW to Montagu, 6 June 1752: 'Mr. Bentley is with me, finishing the drawings for Gray's *Odes*; there are some mandarin-cats fishing for goldfish which will delight you.'

Gray to HW, 8 July 1752: 'I am surprised at the print [Grignion's engraving of Bentley's tail-piece for the *Elegy*], which far surpasses my idea of London graving. . . . Mr. Bentley (I believe) will catch a better idea of Stoke House from any old barn he sees, than from my sketch; but I will try my skill.' The drawing that Gray sent is preserved in HW's copy of the book, now WSL; it was reproduced in *Correspondence of Thomas Gray*, ed. Toynbee and Whibley, 1935, i.363.

Gray to HW, July 1752: 'I do not wonder at Dodsley [who thought the plan too elaborate for so slender a body of verse]. You have talked to him of six *odes*. . . . He has reason to gulp when he finds one of them only a long story. . . .

Mrs Vesey

DESIGNS
BY
Mr. R. BENTLEY,
FOR SIX
POEMS
BY
Mr. T. GRAY.

LONDON:
Printed for R. DODSLEY, in Pall-mall.

MDCCLIII.

42. REDUCED. WIDTH OF ORIGINAL 14.6 cm.

EDITORIAL CONTRIBUTIONS BY WALPOLE

Pray, when the fine book is to be printed, let me revise the press, for you know you can't; and there are a few trifles I could wish altered. . . . My compliments to Mr. Bentley.'

HW to Montagu, 28 August 1752: 'The Poemata Grayo-Bentleiana . . . are in great forwardness, and I trust will appear this winter.'

Gray to HW, 17 December 1752: 'I sent to Dodsley some time since, who wrote to me by your order, what little alterations I had to make. . . . He tells me now, he could finish in a fortnight, if I were in town, but this would be very inconvenient to me at present; so I must have the sheets sent me to correct hither, and I suppose it may come out in less than a month. . . . I have just received the first proofs from Dodsley. I thought it was to be a quarto, but it is a little folio. The stanzas are numbered, which I do not like.' The numbering of the stanzas was eliminated.

Gray to Dodsley, 12 February 1753: 'I am not at all satisfied with the title. To have it conceived that I publish a Collection of *Poems* (half a dozen little matters . . .) thus pompously adorned would make me appear very justly ridiculous. I desire it may be understood . . . that the verses are only subordinate, and explanatory to the drawings. . . . I shall be contented with three copies. . . . I will again put down the title: Designs by Mr. R. Bentley for Six Poems of Mr. T. Gray.' Presumably Dodsley's proposed title had read: Poems by T. Gray, etc. HW replied to Gray's complaint, 20 February 1753.

Gray's next worry was Dodsley's plan to prefix an engraving by Müller of Eckhardt's portrait. Dodsley felt that half a guinea was a high price for so slim a book, and that a fine portrait would help to justify or excuse the price (HW to Gray, 20 Feb. 1753). But when Gray saw a proof of the portrait, he wrote to HW, 13 February 1753: 'Sure you are not out of your wits! This I know, if you suffer my head to be printed, you infallibly will put me out of mine. I conjure you immediately to put a stop to any such design. . . . I am extremely in earnest. . . . I had wrote to Dodsley to tell him how little I liked the title he had prefixed, but your letter has put all that out of my head. If you think it necessary to print these "Explanations" for the use of people that have no eyes, I could be glad they were a little altered.' HW preserved a proof of the suppressed portrait in his own copy of the book, and Gray and Kirgate did likewise; a number of other copies are known.

Bentley's drawings were faithfully engraved by Johann Sebastian Müller (*or* Miller) and by Charles Grignion. HW pasted the full set of completed drawings in a copy of the book, in place of the engravings. He preserved two preliminary sketches (the tail-piece for the 'Long Story') in his scrapbook of Bentley's drawings, now WSL. Kirgate, who did not come to SH until 1765, managed to adorn his own copy of the book, now WSL, with four of Bentley's sketches and several proofs.

The book is properly regarded as a landmark in the history of English book-illustration, although it has recently been described in print as 'quaint and sometimes greatly overrated.' But the best of Bentley's drawings for the 'Ode on the Death of Selima' seem to me in their ironic incongruity imaginatively suited to Gray's mock-heroic lines. If Gray's 'Stanzas to Mr. Bentley' were sincere, we must at least grant that he was delighted by the drawings, however dubious he may have been about his own poems. The book was handsome, however expensive. Griffiths wrote in the *Monthly Review* for July, 1753: 'We have now before us one of the most elegant publications that our country hath produced for some years past: whether we consider the beauty of the printing, the genius that appears in the designs for the cuts, or the masterly execution of most of the engravings. Nor will the connoisseur in prints, we are persuaded, think the price . . . too high: whatever may be the judgment of the mere poetical purchaser, to whom it may appear somewhat rare to pay half a guinea for thirty-six pages of verse.' The volume seems likely to continue to attract collectors of Gray and connoisseurs of prints, who will not think it 'rare to pay half a guinea for thirty-six pages of verse.' Indeed, it has recently received praise from Sir Kenneth Clark and other critics.

Despite the doubts of publisher and reviewer, three editions were soon needed (see STATES AND VARIANTS below), and new editions were published in 1765 and 1766. James Dodsley then felt that the plates had served their purpose, for Gray wrote to HW, 25 February 1768: 'Dodsley told me in the spring [of 1767] that the plates from Mr. Bentley's designs were worn out, and he wanted to have them copied and reduced . . . for a new edition. I dissuaded him. . . .' So Dodsley published Gray's *Poems* in 1768 without illustration, but after Gray's death Bentley's plates were republished in 1775 and 1789.

Folio (actually imperial quarto printed in half-sheets, but cut so that its proportions make it look like a folio. See Gray's letter, 17 December 1752, quoted above. Dodsley's advertisement describes it as royal quarto); published by Dodsley, 29 March 1753, at 10/6 sewed. Approximately 39.5 x 28 cm. uncut.

Twenty half-sheets, printed without signatures.

Pagination: Half-title and title-page, with versos blank; [i–iv] HW's Explanation of the Prints (often bound at end); [1]–[36] (numbered leaves, with versos blank) text.

Six plates.

STATES AND VARIANTS

There are three distinct editions dated 1753, but since the wording of the title-page is identical in all three and all three have been sold as first editions, it seems easier to describe the editions and discriminate among them as if they were different states. There are no special copies on large paper or on thick paper, despite frequent descriptions of such copies in catalogues; but an untrimmed copy has very wide margins and an unpressed one may seem unusually bulky. Dodsley's advertisement in the *Daily Advertiser* describes the book precisely: 'Elegantly printed in royal quarto; Price sewed 10/6.'

1. The first of the three editions can be identified readily by the half-title, which reads: 'Drawings, &c.' In all other editions the half-title is, more correctly, 'Designs, &c.' On page 28 of the first edition the heading reads: 'ELEGY / Written in a Country Church Yard.' In all other editions the heading reads: 'ELEGY / WRITTEN IN A / COUNTRY CHURCH YARD.' The three rows of printer's flowers in the Explanation of the Prints are uniform in the first edition. A number of smaller typographical points are peculiar to the first edition, but they are not especially significant.*

This edition is established as the first by HW's two copies, described below. There are also at Farmington three other copies of this edition, inscribed respectively: 'Edw. Mathew 1753'; 'Mrs. Vesey'; 'Given by Horace Walpole to the Count St. Germain and by him to the Marquis St. Simon 1754.' Other copies of this edition are in the British Museum, Library of Congress, Boston Public Library, Harvard, Michigan, and University of Rochester. I purchased a good but broken-backed copy for $11 in 1944, not to establish it as the 'genuine first' but to use it in teaching. A facsimile of the title-page was published in the *second* edition of Austin Lane Poole's *Poems of Gray*, 1926, and also in A. F. Bell's edition of Gray's *Poems*, 1915.

2. Discrimination between the other two editions dated 1753 is simple enough, but their order is not certainly established. The book must have been unexpectedly popular, since there are separate dated editions, not variant issues, in 1765 and 1766. If two editions were then called for, twelve years after the first edition, it is not hard to believe that Dodsley may have reprinted twice in 1753 or 1754. Dr. Johnson says in the 'Life of Gray': 'I believe the poems and the plates recommended each other so highly that the whole impression was soon bought.' I have found no advertisements after the customary few in-

* Mr. R. Fukuhara, in his *Bibliographical Study of Thomas Gray*, published in Japanese in 1933, noticed that the half-title was 'Drawings' in some copies and 'Designs' in others, but I think he did not perceive that they were entirely distinct editions.

A facsimile of the title-page is in all three editions of Austin Lane Poole's *Poems of Gray*, but the publisher prepared a new plate each time; by the curious operation of bibliographical chance in the selection of copies, these three plates reproduce the three different printings dated 1753.

sertions when the book was first published, but the existence of three independent printings dated 1753 seems conclusive evidence. Furthermore, if Gray wrote his bibliographical note on the margin of the *Pembroke MS* (reprinted in Lane Poole's edition of the *Poems* and elsewhere) before 1765, and I believe from its arrangement with insertions that most of it was certainly written before 1759, his reference to the *Designs* 'of which there is a 2d edition' means that he knew of the first reprinting. There can be no question of piracy, since all editions use the same plates; and since I can find no hint that these reprints were prepared after Dodsley's death in 1764 to deceive collectors, I believe all three editions were printed in 1753 or 1754.

What I think is the second edition has the same rows of printer's flowers, in HW's Explanation of the Prints, as the first edition; but in the rows on the third and fourth pages an exclamation point is inserted. In setting page 26 the compositor ran out of the letter 'd' and so used an inverted 'p' for the letter 'd' the last seven times on the page.

In placing this edition second, I reverse the order I suggested in the *Times Literary Supplement*, 3 February 1945. The paper seems identical in this edition and the first; slightly different in the third. Typographically, these two editions are closely related, whereas the third edition introduces some dozen new readings (mere variants of spelling or capitalization). The reprint of 1765 agrees generally with the first two editions, and was presumably set up from one or the other. The reprint of 1766, on the other hand, reproduces about half of the new readings in the third edition and was perhaps set up from it.

Copies of this second edition seem about as plentiful as the first edition. I have examined copies at Columbia (Typographical Library), the New York Public Library, the Morgan Library, the Newberry Library, the University of Chicago, Harvard and Yale. Buxton Forman's copy, now WSL, has the head-piece to the *Elegy* inverted, on page 28—not perhaps an astonishing variant in a hastily reprinted edition. A facsimile of the title-page of this edition was published in the *first* edition of Austin Lane Poole's *Poems of Gray*, 1917.

3. The third edition seems to be distinctly less common. One copy is in the Spencer Collection of the New York Public Library, and another copy is at Farmington. In this printing the half-title and the heading on page 28 agree with the second edition; but page 26 uses a

EDITORIAL CONTRIBUTIONS BY WALPOLE

correct 'd' throughout and in the Explanation of the Prints one smaller piece is inserted in each row of printer's flowers (an exclamation point in the second edition). A facsimile of the title-page was published in the *third* edition of Austin Lane Poole's *Poems of Gray*, 1937.

OTHER EDITIONS

1765. The six poems are printed on one side of the sheet as in the editions of 1753, but at the end are the two *Odes* of 1757, printed on both sides. I have seen a copy of this edition, owned in 1944 by the Brick Row Book Shop, in which the tail-piece on page 27 is printed upside down.

1766. Similar to the edition of 1765; but the text is closer to the third printing dated 1753 (see STATES AND VARIANTS above). The tail-piece on page 55, at the end of 'The Bard,' was first used in this edition.

The editions of 1775 and 1789 are close reprints, with only very minor typographical changes. The edition of 1789 is on somewhat thinner paper, and not quite so tall.

In 1756 the text of the *Six Poems,* without Bentley's illustrations, was reprinted in Dublin. Gosse's copy, described in Northup's *Bibliography of Thomas Gray,* is now at Yale.

COPIES

1. HW's copy, with his annotations; proof of Eckhardt-Müller portrait of Gray. Listed in *Description of SH* as 'bound in marble and gilt,' but now rebound in red levant morocco by Rivière and Son. SH Sale, iii.193, to Thorpe, £3.10.0 (with three other books); Sotheby's, 1 July 1924 (MacGeorge Sale), lot 652, to Maggs, £36; Freeman, 23 March 1936 (C. T. Jeffery Sale), lot 179, to Rosenbach for WSL, $400.

2. HW's copy, with his MS note on fly-leaf, and with Bentley's original drawings mounted in place of the engravings; Gray's rough sketch of Stoke inserted. HW kept this volume in the Glass Closet in his library. Original red morocco; bookplate of Laurence Currie. SH Sale, vii.54 (London Sale, lot 1044), to Bohn for Beckford, £8.8.0; Sotheby's, 3 July 1882 (Beckford Sale, Part 1), lot 802, to Ellis and White, £20; Maggs, November 1933, to WSL, £230.

3. Gray's copy, with HW's note on proof of Eckhardt-Müller portrait, and Gray's autograph MSS (the *Progress of Poesy* and extra stanza of the *Elegy*) bound in. Sotheby's, 28 August 1851 (Penn Sale), lot 143, to Stephens, £2.18.0; Sotheby's, 22 July 1864 (George Daniel Sale), lot 738, to Harvey, £30. Rebound in morocco by Rivière with arms of W. A. Fraser on sides; Sotheby's, 22 April 1901 (Fraser Sale), lot 754, to Sabin, £400; Sotheby's, 11 December 1913 (Library of an American amateur [Hoe]), lot 67, to Martin, £420.

4. Presentation copy to Count St. Germain, inscribed on title-page: 'Given by Horace Walpole to the Count St. Germain, and by him to the Marquis St. Simon 1754, both friends of him.' Original vellum. Purchased by WSL, in 1944.

5. William Cole's copy, with his MS notes; calf by Kalthoeber. Offered by B. White, 1784 (Cole Library), lot 150, £1.11.6; Sotheby's, 26 October 1916 (Col. Prideaux Sale), lot 1283, to Quaritch, £1.

6. Thomas Kirgate's copy, containing mixed sheets of the editions of 1775 and 1789, with his MS annotations; now bound in red morocco by Rivière and Son. Extra-illustrated with four of Bentley's preliminary drawings and several proofs, a proof of the Eckhardt-Müller portrait of Gray, and prints of numerous other portraits; also MS memoranda by Gray and two letters (one in Kirgate's hand) by HW. A copy of Gray's *Odes*, 1757, was removed by Rosenbach in 1934. King and Lochée, 4 December 1810 (Kirgate Sale), lot 406, to Baker, £5.12.6; Sotheby's, 8 June 1825 (Baker Sale), lot 836, to Upcott, £3.13.6; Sotheby's, 3 May 1895 (Framingham Sale), lot 394, to Pearson, £5.10.0; Rosenbach, September 1934, to WSL, $350.

43. CATALOGUE OF PICTURES OF CHARLES THE FIRST. 1757.

'Short Notes': '10 June [1757] was published a Catalogue of the collection of pictures of Charles the First, to which I had written a little introduction. I afterwards wrote short prefaces or advertisements in the same manner to the Catalogues of the collections of James the Second and the Duke of Buckingham.'

The catalogue was made by Abraham Van Der Dort, keeper of King Charles's collections, and prepared for the press by George Vertue. HW wrote in his Advertisement [introduction]: '. . . transcribed by . . . Mr. Vertue . . . and was by him prepared for the press, part of it being actually printed off before his death.' Vertue died 24 July 1756.

The publisher Bathoe bought the MSS of the three catalogues at Vertue's Sale, 18 March 1757, and prepared them for printing. HW needed only to look over the MSS and write his short introductions. The three introductions are reprinted in the *Works*, 1798.

Quarto in half-sheets; published 10 June 1757 by Bathoe, at 10/6.
Signatures: One leaf; a²; B–3E²; 3F¹.
Pagination: Title-page, with verso blank; i–iv HW's Advertisement; [1]–182 text; 183–202 Index.

STATES AND VARIANTS

The paper changes after p. 108, and it seems reasonably certain that Vertue had printed the first 108 pages.

Some copies have inserted after HW's Advertisement eight pages

CATALOGUE
AND
DESCRIPTION
of King CHARLES the FIRST's
CAPITAL COLLECTION

OF

PICTURES,	BRONZES,
LIMNINGS,	MEDALS, and
STATUES,	Other CURIOSITIES;

Now first published from an ORIGINAL MANUSCRIPT in the ASHMOLEAN MUSÆUM at OXFORD.

The whole transcribed and prepared for the PRESS, and a great part of it printed, by the late ingenious Mr. VERTUE, and now finished from his Papers.

LONDON,

Printed for W. BATHOE, at his Circulating Library near *Exeter Change*, in the *Strand*.
MDCCLVII.

43.

of 'Pictures belonging to King Charles the First at his several palaces, appraised; and most of them sold by the Council of State,' signed A–B². This inventory, drawn up in 1649, was probably printed soon after the *Catalogue* had been completed. Bathoe's advertisement of the catalogues published by him, printed at the end of the *Catalogue of the Duke of Buckingham's Pictures* in 1759, lists a second edition that includes the inventory of 1649; since I have never seen such an edition, I judge that the inventory was merely inserted in unsold copies of the first edition.

A copy in the SH Sale, iv.170, was described as 'large paper, uncut, very rare.' I have no other knowledge of copies on large paper.

44. CATALOGUE OF THE PICTURES BELONGING TO JAMES THE SECOND. 1758.

The Catalogue was made by W. Chiffinch, and prepared for the press by Vertue. Vertue himself made the Catalogue of Queen Caroline's pictures, which are part of the volume. For general notes on the catalogues, see the *Catalogue of Charles the First* above.

Quarto in half-sheets; published in April 1758 by Bathoe, at 10/6.
Signatures: One half-sheet, unsigned; B–Oo²; *A–*N².
Pagination: [i] title-page; [ii] blank; iii–iv HW's Advertisement; [1]–109 text; 110–144 Indexes; [1]–31 Queen Caroline's pictures; 32–46 Index; 47–51 Pictures at Kensington; [52] advertisements. There are four double plates.

The set-off in Signature Z suggests that it was reprinted just before publication—a cancel half-sheet.

45. CATALOGUE OF THE PICTURES BELONGING TO THE DUKE OF BUCKINGHAM. 1759.

For general notes on the catalogues, see the *Catalogue of Charles the First* above.

Quarto in half-sheets; published in July 1759 by Bathoe, at 6/–.
Signatures: One half-sheet, unsigned; B–X². Signature M is signed L in error.
Pagination: [i] title-page; [ii] blank; [iii–iv] HW's Advertisement; [1]–79 text; [80] advertisements.

A
CATALOGUE
OF THE

COLLECTION of PICTURES, &c.

BELONGING TO

King JAMES the Second;

To which is added,

A CATALOGUE

Of the PICTURES and DRAWINGS

In the CLOSET of

The late Queen CAROLINE,

With their exact MEASURES;

And also of the PRINCIPAL PICTURES in the Palace at
KENSINGTON.

LONDON,

Printed for W. BATHOE, at his Circulating Library near *Exeter Change*, in the *Strand*. MDCCLVIII.

A CATALOGUE

Of the Curious

COLLECTION of PICTURES

OF

GEORGE VILLIERS, Duke of BUCKINGHAM.

In which is included

The valuable Collection of Sir PETER PAUL RUBENS.

WITH

The LIFE of GEORGE VILLIERS, Duke of Buckingham,
The celebrated Poet.

Written by BRIAN FAIRFAX, Esq;
And never before published.

ALSO,

A Catalogue of Sir PETER LELY's capital Collection of Pictures, Statues, Bronzes, &c. with the exact Measures of the Pictures in both Collections:

A Description of EASTON-NESTON in NORTHAMPTONSHIRE, the Seat of the Right Honourable the Earl of POMFRET; with an Account of the curious antique Statues, Busto's, Urns, &c:

A Description of the CARTOONS at HAMPTON-COURT:

A Letter from Mr. I. TALMAN to Dr. ALDRICH, Dean of Christ-Church, giving an Account of a fine Collection of DRAWINGS of Monsignor MARCHETTI, Bishop of AREZZO; collected by the celebrated Father RESTA.

LONDON:
Printed for W. BATHOE, at his Circulating Library, near EXETER-CHANGE,
in the STRAND.
M DCC LVIII.

45. REDUCED. WIDTH OF ORIGINAL 12.6 cm.

EDITORIAL CONTRIBUTIONS BY WALPOLE

COPIES

It is convenient to record copies of the three catalogues together, since they so frequently occur together. A fourth volume, the *Description of the Works of Hollar* published by Vertue in 1745, is frequently counted as part of the set; a second edition of it was edited by Richard Gough in 1759.

1. HW's set of the four volumes, bound in vellum; SH Sale, iv.157–60, to Rodwell, £22.1.0.

2. A set presented by HW in December 1760 to Lord Bute for the King; now at Windsor Castle.

3. Upcott's set of three volumes, with his name 'William Upcott 1822' on flyleaf of the *Catalogue of Charles the First*. Evans, 18 June 1846 (Upcott Sale), lot 1092; rebound much later in red morocco by Rivière; Sawyer, 1926, to WSL, £15.15.0.

4. Gray's set of three volumes, with his MS notes; red morocco by Clarke and Bedford. Sotheby's, 28 August 1851 (Penn Sale), lot 126, £8.0.0; Sotheby's, 1 May 1884 (Hamilton Sale), lot 2044; Sotheby's 30 June 1933 (Rosebery Sale), lot 1251, to Newton, £33.

5. *Catalogue of Charles I* and *Catalogue of Duke of Buckingham* in one volume; half calf, rebacked; a few MS notes by HW, and additional notes and corrections in another hand. Spurr and Swift, March 1932, to WSL, £5.5.0.

6. James Bindley's set of three catalogues, rebound in one volume, with his note dated 1772; now in the Merritt Collection at Harvard. The set of four volumes was sold by Evans, 5 August 1820 (Bindley Sale, Part 4), lot 796, to Moltens, £4.

7. HW's copy, with his notes, of *Catalogue of Charles I*, described as on large paper, uncut. SH Sale, iv.170, to Boone, £2.8.0; apparently the same copy was sold at Sotheby's, 8 November 1866 (Wellesley Sale), lot 48, and again at Sotheby's in 1881.

8. HW's copy, with his notes, of *Catalogue of James II* was offered by Quaritch in 1909 for £21, and sold in 1919. Messrs. Quaritch first offered this copy for sale in 1883.

9. HW's copy, with his notes, of *Catalogue of the Duke of Buckingham* is now in the British Museum.

10. Thomas Kirgate's copy of *Catalogue of the Duke of Buckingham* was sold at Sotheby's, 30 June 1905 (Miscellaneous Sale), to Ellis, £1.2.0.

46. HENTZNER'S JOURNEY INTO ENGLAND. 1757.

HW furnished the ten-page 'Advertisement.' For description see the *SH Bibliography*, p. 31.

47. HENRY HYDE, LORD CORNBURY, THE MISTAKES. 1758.

'Short Notes': 'About the same time [April 1758] Mrs. Porter published Lord

THE
MISTAKES;
OR, THE
Happy Resentment.
A
COMEDY.

By the late Lord * * * *

LONDON:

Printed by S. RICHARDSON, in the Year 1758.

EDITORIAL CONTRIBUTIONS BY WALPOLE

Hyde's play, to which I had written the advertisement.' The play had been given to Mrs. Porter, to be printed and sold for her benefit.

The book is recorded in the *SH Bibliography,* p. 143, because it has been erroneously considered a product of the SH Press. HW's only contribution was the advertisement, along with a subscription. The advertisement is reprinted in the *Works*.

Baker's *Companion to the Playhouse* says Mrs. Porter distributed three thousand copies at 5/- each, and the list of subscribers accounts for just over three thousand copies. The number of subscribers who are put down for four copies is somewhat extraordinary. Some sixteen, including HW, are down for twenty-one copies each; Earl Cowper is listed for twenty-one and the Countess Cowper for eighty; John Spencer, Esq. is listed for one hundred twenty copies. I do not know that any copies were sold through the booksellers; I judge that copies were priced at 5/- so that anybody who subscribed five guineas was automatically assigned twenty-one copies, and others in proportion—four copies to a pound. The book cannot be considered rare to-day.

Royal octavo in half-sheets.
Signatures: One leaf; a–b^4; c^2; B–L^4; M^3.
Pagination: Title-page, with verso blank; [i]–xvi List of subscribers; [xvii–xviii] HW's Advertisement; [xix] Prologue; [xx] Dramatis Personae; [1]–83 text; [84–85] Epilogue; [86] blank.
The title-page appears to have been printed with Signature M.

States and Variants

A copy on large paper is recorded in the British Museum's *Catalogue,* but it is on the same royal paper that is used in all copies I have examined.

I have seen two copies in which some signatures (B–D in both, and H in one copy) have been reset; it seems likely that this does not indicate a new issue, but a reprinting of a few signatures when the subscription list grew beyond expectation. In addition to numerous small differences in text, the reprinted signatures can be identified by the head-piece on p. 20 (a cherub's head with wings), whereas in the first printing the head-piece on p. 20 is the same as that used for Acts 3, 4, and 5; in the reprinted Signature H the tail-piece on p. 52 is an urn, whereas in the first printing the tail-piece is the same bearded head as that used for Acts 2, 4, and 5. There seems no doubt, bibliographically, that the first printing is the one in which the head- and tail-pieces are uniform.

COPIES

1. Mr. Francis Edwards in 1913 offered for sale the author's presentation copy to Mrs. Porter.

2. A copy described as having a name on title and presentation inscription on fly-leaf was sold at the American Art Association, 7 January 1927 (Isham Sale), lot 24, $5.

3. HW's copy was bought at the SH Sale, vi.29, by Dr. Philip Bliss of Oxford.

48. WHITWORTH'S ACCOUNT OF RUSSIA. 1758.

HW furnished the 'Advertisement.' For description see the *SH Bibliography*, p. 42.

49. BENTLEY'S REFLECTIONS ON CRUELTY. 1759.

'Short Notes': '22 November [1758] was published a pamphlet written by Mr. R. Bentley, called *Reflections on the Different Ideas of the French and English with Regard to Cruelty*. It was designed to promote a bill (that I meditated) of perpetual insolvency. I wrote the dedication. It was *not* printed at Strawberry Hill.' In a note in the *Waldegrave MS*, HW says much the same thing.

Isaac Reed's note in his copy (now WSL): 'This pamphlet was written by the late Horace Earl of Orford. The original copy in his own hand writing is now in the possession of Mr. Bedford. It was printed by means of Mr. Bedford's father who was deputy to Lord Orford as Usher of the Exchequer and intimate with the Tonsons. It was the custom of Lord Orford to employ this gentleman to get pamphlets [etc.?] printed for him which he did not wish to be known as the author. Several proofs of this are now in Mr. Bedford's possession. . . . Mr. Bedford Senr. collected the present piece and others (most of which I believe to have been Lord Orford's) into a volume.' HW was the author of the dedication only, not of the whole pamphlet; but most of Reed's note, written in 1801, seems accurate. The copy in HW's hand, however, if it was owned by Charles Bedford in 1801, has not been traced.

Reed was not the only man who, knowing HW had something to do with Bentley's pamphlet, named HW as the author. Kirgate, in a note written for Richard Bull and now preserved in the Huntington Library, includes it in a list of three anonymous pieces he assigns to HW.

Octavo in half-sheets; approximately 22.2 x 13.5 cm. uncut; published at sixpence, 22 November 1758, with title-page dated 1759.
Signatures: [A]–E⁴.
Pagination: [1] half-title; [2] blank; [3] title-page; [4] blank; [5–6] Dedication by HW, signed 'Unknown'; [7]–39 text; [40] blank.

COPIES

1. Isaac Reed's copy, with his MS note; half calf, uncut; half-title wanting.

REFLECTIONS

ON THE

DIFFERENT IDEAS

OF THE

FRENCH and *ENGLISH*,

In regard to C<small>RUELTY</small>;

WITH

Some Hints for improving our Humanity in a particular Branch.

By a Man.

LONDON:

Printed for J. and R. T<small>ONSON</small> in the Strand.
MDCCLIX.

49.

King and Lochée, 18 November 1807 (Reed Sale), lot 3279 (sold with Hayter's *Essay on Liberty of the Press*), 6/–; in Lord Carlingford's collection, with his bookplate, and then in Lord Strachie's collection; Lord Strachie, December 1943, to WSL, in a collection.

There is a good, rebound copy with half-title at the John Crerar Library in Chicago. The printed catalogue of the British Museum lists two copies under 'Man' [from the title-page], and by a queer cataloguing error ascribes the book to Horace Walpole, 5th Earl of Orford.

50. LIFE OF EDWARD LORD HERBERT OF CHERBURY. 1764.

HW wrote the Dedication and 'Advertisement,' and edited the whole MS. For description see the *SH Bibliography*, p. 68.

51. POEMS BY ANNA CHAMBER COUNTESS TEMPLE. 1764.

HW furnished the complimentary verses to Lady Temple. For description see the *SH Bibliography*, pp. 72–77.

On p. 76, Copy 9, marked by HW 'The only copy I have left,' was sold by Scribner's to Robert Hartshorne; at the Hartshorne Sale, 3 November 1945, it was purchased by WSL for $55. Properly enough, Signature F of this copy is in the second state. Richard Bull's copy in red morocco, sold by Lewis Buddy in 1909, was purchased privately by WSL in August 1944 for $50; in this copy Signature F is likewise in the second state.

Another slight variant of Signature F was offered for sale by Peter Murray Hill in 1945 and is now WSL.

52. HOYLAND'S POEMS. 1769.

HW furnished the 'Advertisement.' For description see the *SH Bibliography*, p. 85.

53. JAMES GRANGER'S BIOGRAPHICAL HISTORY. 1769–74.

HW to William Cole, 20 August 1768: 'Mr. Granger is printing his laborious and curious catalogue of English heads. . . .'

Granger's *Letters*, published in 1805 by J. P. Malcolm, show how assiduously he sought for help, especially for his *Supplement*. He spent some seven years on his materials, and asked HW to read his MS in 1764. William Cole, among many, wrote Granger repeatedly after 1768, enclosing notes and advice. Davies the publisher wrote Granger, 4 February 1769, to say that the book was twice as long as Hamilton, the printer, had at first calculated; hence the decision to print each volume in two parts. Davies also recorded a good deal of the printing and

A BIOGRAPHICAL HISTORY OF ENGLAND,

FROM

EGBERT the GREAT to the REVOLUTION:

CONSISTING OF

CHARACTERS difposed in different CLASSES, and adapted to a METHODICAL CATALOGUE of Engraved BRITISH HEADS.

INTENDED AS

An ESSAY towards reducing our BIOGRAPHY to SYSTEM, and a Help to the Knowledge of PORTRAITS.

INTERSPERSED WITH

Variety of ANECDOTES, and MEMOIRS of a great Number of PERSONS, not to be found in any other Biographical Work.

With a PREFACE, fhewing the Utility of a Collection of ENGRAVED PORTRAITS to fupply the Defect, and anfwer the various Purpofes, of MEDALS.

By the Rev. J. GRANGER, Vicar of Shiplake, in Oxfordfhire.

Animam pictura pafcit inani.   VIRG.
Celebrare domeftica facta.   HOR.

VOL. I.

LONDON,
Printed for T. DAVIES, in Ruffel-Street, Covent-Garden. 1769.

A SUPPLEMENT,

CONSISTING OF

Corrections and large Additions,

TO A

BIOGRAPHICAL HISTORY of ENGLAND,

Referred to their proper Places in that Work:

TO WHICH,

Besides an INDEX to the ADDITIONAL CHARACTERS,

ARE SUBJOINED

Exact EMENDATIONS and IMPROVEMENTS of the INDEX
to the FORMER VOLUMES;

AND A

LIST of CURIOUS PORTRAITS of EMINENT PERSONS
not yet engraved,

Communicated, by the Honourable HORACE WALPOLE, to the Author,

JAMES GRANGER,

VICAR of SHIPLAKE, in OXFORDSHIRE.

LONDON,
Printed for T. DAVIES, Ruffel-Street, Covent-Garden; J. ROBSON, New Bond-Street;
G. ROBINSON, Pater-noster-Row; T. BECKET, T. CADELL, and T. EVANS, Strand.
MDCCLXXIV.

53. SUPPLEMENT.

EDITORIAL CONTRIBUTIONS BY WALPOLE

publishing history: the whole edition seems to have been 750 copies; in July 1769 no more than 300 sets were unsold; in October about 160, and 40 of the sets printed on one side, were unsold; in February 1770 there were 140 and 20 sets, respectively. By March, when he had had returns from booksellers, however, Davies estimated that at least 240 copies were still unsold, and plans for printing a new edition were therefore delayed. The work sold well enough, though slowly, and Granger made a profit of £400 in the first two years after publication.

HW to William Cole, 27 May 1769: 'Mr. Granger has published his catalogue of prints and lives down to the Revolution, and as the work sells well, I believe, nay, do not doubt but we shall have the rest [the continuation]. There are a few copies printed but on one side of the leaf. As I know you love scribbling in such books as well as I do, I beg you will give me leave to make you a present of one set. I shall send it in about a week to Mr. Gray, and have desired him, as soon as he has turned it over, to convey it to you. I have found a few mistakes, and you will find more. To my mortification, though I have four thousand heads, I find upon a rough calculation that I still shall want three or four hundred.'

HW read and annotated the MS, and Granger says in his Preface: 'My thanks are in a particular manner due to Mr. Walpole, who with his own hand did me the honour to add to the catalogue a description of many heads not found in Mr. West's collection.' Cole in thanking HW for his present says: 'I shall forever value them the more . . . for your polishing part of them, for I am pretty clear I see your pencil in some parts of them.'

The dedication to HW is briefly appropriate. See HW to Cole, 14 June 1769: 'I did my utmost to dissuade Mr. Granger from the dedication, and took especial pains to get *my virtues* left out of the question; till I found he would be quite hurt if I did not let him express his gratitude. . . .'

HW to Mann, 6 May 1770: 'Another rage is for prints of English portraits. . . . Lately, I assisted a clergyman in compiling a catalogue of them; since the publication, scarce heads in books, not worth threepence, will sell for five guineas.'

Supplement

Davies to Granger, 27 October 1770: 'I heartily wish your *Supplement* were ready to put to the press. I cannot publish an edition of your book in octavo before the other has been offered to the publick. I am determined to print the octavo edition immediately after the quarto *Supplement* has made its appearance.' He did just this; or rather, he printed the second edition in 1774 but delayed its publication until 1775. Cadell and others shared in publishing the *Supplement*.

HW to Mason, 8 December 1773: 'Mr. Granger teases me to correct catalogues of prints.'

HW to Sir John Fenn, 17 September 1774: 'Mr. Granger, I see by the papers, has published his *Supplement*. I have not yet received it. I am sorry his bookseller has quoted me for the list of unengraved portraits. It did not deserve such parade.'

HW to Cole, 11 October 1774: 'Have you seen Mr. Granger's *Supplement?*

BIBLIOGRAPHY OF HORACE WALPOLE

Methinks it grows too diffuse.' Davies the publisher had also been alarmed by Granger's diffuseness; see Granger to HW, 30 January 1772: 'As Mr. Davies is desirous of printing the *Supplement . . . with all expedition,* I am emboldened . . . to beg the favour of you to cast an eye over the papers that accompany this letter, before they go to the press.' Presumably this letter was prompted by a letter from Davies to Granger, 5 November 1771: 'I begin to be impatient for your *Supplement:* I am afraid you are too solicitous to make improvements, and to collect additional matter.'

After Granger's death in 1776, his MSS were purchased by Lord Mountstuart. James Boswell, at Lord Mountstuart's request, wrote to Dr. Johnson to inquire about a possible editor for the materials. In 1806 the Rev. Mark Noble did make use of the MSS in editing his continuation of Granger.

It was Granger's work that encouraged the style of extra-illustrating and gave it the name of Grangerizing.

In a note on pp. 219–20 of the first volume Granger told the story of HW's narrow escape at Dr. Mead's Sale, when his unlimited commission to Graham on Winstanley's *Plans of Audley End* was run up to £49; see HW to Bentley, 13 December 1754.

Two volumes in four parts, and *Supplement* of 1774; post quarto; published 16 May 1769, two guineas in boards (the *Supplement* in September 1774 was priced at 18/– in boards); an untrimmed copy measures approximately 24.5 x 19 cm.

Signatures: Vol. I, Part 1. One plate; [A]⁴; a–b⁴; B–Nn⁴.

Vol. I, Part 2. Half-sheet unsigned; B–Pp⁴; Qq².

Vol. II, Part 1. Half-sheet unsigned; inserted slip; B–Qq⁴.

Vol. II, Part 2. Half-sheet unsigned; B–Rr⁴.

Supplement. Half-sheet unsigned; B–3Y⁴; 3Z².

Pagination: Vol. I, Part 1. Portrait frontispiece; title-page, with verso blank; Errata in Vol. I, with verso blank; Dedication to HW, 3 pp., with verso of second leaf blank; Plan of the Catalogue, 2 pp.; Preface, 13 pp.; Note, 1 p.; [1]–280 text.

Vol. I, Part 2. One blank leaf, conjugate with title-page; title-page, with verso blank; [281]–580 text.

Vol. II, Part 1. Title-page, with verso blank; Errata in Vol. II, with verso blank; inserted slip containing 'Addend. to the Errata' (frequently lacking); [1]–303 text; [304] blank.

Vol. II, Part 2. One blank leaf, conjugate with title-page; title-page, with verso blank; [305]–567 text; [568] blank; Index, 47 pp.; Advertisement, 1 p.

Supplement. Title-page ('A Supplement, consisting of corrections and large additions . . . and a List of curious portraits of eminent persons not yet engraved, communicated by the Honourable Horace Walpole'), with verso blank; Advertisement, 2 pp.; [1]–533 text, additions, index; 534–[547, i.e., 539] List of portraits not engraved, communicated by HW; [540] Advertisement of Granger's Sermons.

STATES AND VARIANTS

A few copies of the original volumes, priced at three guineas, were printed on one side only, 'for the convenience of such gentlemen as may chuse to place the heads near to the lives,' or, as the advertisements suggested, 'such gentlemen as chuse to cut the volumes to pieces, and affix the separate characters to the backs of the prints, or bind them up with them.' (Except for the preliminary leaves, therefore, each gathering of these copies comprises two quired sheets.) It was such a set that HW sent to Cole, and his own set described below is likewise printed on one side only.

EDITIONS

The second edition, incorporating the *Supplement,* was published in 1775, four volumes in octavo. (Twenty sets were printed on one side of the paper only.) The third edition was published in 1779; the fourth in 1804 with an Appendix of additional matter; and the fifth in six volumes in 1824. Mark Noble's continuation, *A Biographical History of England, from the Revolution to the End of George I's Reign,* was published in 1806, three volumes in octavo.

The Grangerizing flame was fanned by the publication of Richardson's Collection of Portraits illustrating Granger's *Biographical History,* 1792–1812, and other collections.

COPIES

1. HW's copy, four volumes printed on one side bound in quarter calf, and *Supplement* in boards; uncut. HW's signature and shelf-mark, his bookplate in *Supplement,* lists of prints that he lacked, and his extensive annotations throughout. Modern book label of Charles Bidwell, Ely. SH Sale, iv.7, to Thorpe, £7.17.6; Bowes and Bowes, October 1945, to WSL, £50 (with two volumes of Richardson's Portraits).

2. Another set with annotations on two pages by HW; four volumes, 1769. SH Sale, vii.116 (London Sale, 1095), to Thorpe, 15/–. Now in the Morgan Collection at Princeton.

3. Granger's copy is owned by Dr. L. F. Powell of Oxford.

4. A set extended by about 2000 plates from five to twenty volumes, with specially printed titles; bound in blue morocco about 1813 by C. Smith. Sotheby's, 29 April 1920 (Miscellaneous Sale), lot 8, to Spencer, £22; Sotheby's, 30 June 1930 (Miscellaneous Sale), lot 551, to Halliday, £25; Halliday, March 1936, to WSL, £25. Two similar sets are mentioned in the article on Granger in the *Dictionary of National Biography*.

54. MEMOIRES DU COMTE DE GRAMMONT. 1772.

HW wrote the preface to this new edition. For description see the *SH Bibliography*, p. 96.

55. LETTERS OF EDWARD VI. 1772.

HW wrote the 'Advertisement' in No. 1 and the Life of Wyatt in No. 2. For description see the *SH Bibliography*, p. 99.

56. MISCELLANEOUS ANTIQUITIES. 1772.

HW wrote the 'Advertisement.' For description see the *SH Bibliography*, p. 103.

57. EPILOGUE TO JEPHSON'S BRAGANZA. 1775.

'Short Notes': 'In February 1775 wrote the Epilogue to *Braganza;* and three letters to the author, Mr. Jephson, on Tragedy.'

HW to Lady Ossory, 1 February 1775: 'Mr. Jephson's tragedy . . . exceeded my expectations infinitely. The language is noble. . . . My Irish friends, the Binghams, have overpersuaded me to write an epilogue, which was wanting. They gave me the subject, which I have executed miserably. . . .' See also HW to Mme. du Deffand, 31 January 1775.

HW to Mason, 18 February 1775: '*Braganza* was acted last night with prodigious success. . . . There was an excellent prologue written by Murphy. For my poor epilogue, though well delivered by Mrs. Yates, it appeared to me the flattest thing I ever heard. . . . I wish it could be spoken no more.'

HW to Jephson, 24 February 1775: 'I could not refuse Mr. Tighe's request of writing an epilogue, though I never was a poet, and have done writing—but in excuse I must say I complied, only because an epilogue was immediately wanted. You have by this time, I fear, Sir, seen it in the newspapers: it was written in one evening; I knew it was not only bad, but most unworthy of such a play. . . . I beg your pardon, Sir; I am ashamed of it. . . . For my own part, though so discontent with my epilogue, I shall always be proud of having facilitated and hastened *Braganza's* appearance on the stage by the zeal with which I solicited the licence. . . .'

BRAGANZA.

A TRAGEDY.

PERFORMED AT THE

THEATRE ROYAL

IN

DRURY-LANE.

WRITTEN BY

ROBERT JEPHSON, Esq.

acted for the first time feb. 17th

LONDON:

Printed for T. EVANS, near York-Buildings in the Strand;
AND
T. DAVIES, in Ruffel-Street, Covent-Garden.
MDCCLXXV.
[Price One Shilling and Six-Pence.]

HW to Mason, 7 March 1775: 'Here is *Braganza*. I do not say that either the subject or conduct are interesting. The language is good, the poetry charming.'

The three letters to Jephson were first published in the *Works* of 1798, ii.305–314, where HW planned them as the first work to be added to what he had printed in his lifetime.

Octavo in half-sheets; published by Evans and Davies, 27 February 1775, at 1/6.
Signatures: A–K⁴; L².
Pagination: [i] title-page; [ii] blank; [iii]–iv Dedication; [v–vi] Prologue, by Arthur Murphy; [vii] Epilogue, by a Friend [i.e., HW]; [viii] Persons; [1]–76 text.

EDITIONS

Three editions were published in London in 1775, and the play was reprinted in Dublin. HW's Epilogue was reprinted in the *London Magazine* for March 1775, and in the *Works* of 1798, iv.400.

Although the play represents the first publication of HW's Epilogue in book form, there seems no doubt that the newspapers published it earlier. The *London Chronicle*, 18 February 1775, in reviewing the play, said: 'A sing-song kind of epilogue, written by Mr. Horace Walpole, and spoken by Mrs. Yates, closed the entertainment'; both the *London Chronicle* and the *Public Advertiser* printed the Epilogue 23 February 1775.

COPIES

1. HW's copy is in his collection called *Theatre of George 3*, now WSL.

58. MASON'S EDITION OF GRAY'S POEMS. 1775.

Mason was Gray's chief literary executor, and almost immediately after Gray's death in 1771, he began to prepare an edition of Gray's poems and a biography. HW offered to print such a work at the SH Press, but Mason chose to undertake it as a commercial project. Mason sent to HW all the passages that might be of interest to him, and HW responded with extensive notes and corrections in the proofs. The completed book is the result of Mason's efforts as amended by HW. The few quotations that follow will suffice to indicate the progress of the work.

HW to William Cole, 12 August 1771: 'I am excessively shocked at reading in the papers that Mr. Gray is dead. . . . What writings has he left? Who are his executors? I should earnestly wish, if he has destined anything to the public, to print it at my press.'

THE POEMS OF MR. GRAY.

TO WHICH ARE PREFIXED
MEMOIRS
OF HIS
LIFE and WRITINGS
BY
W. MASON, M.A.

YORK:
Printed by A. Ward; and sold by J. Dodsley, Pall-Mall, London; and J. Todd, Stonegate, York.
MDCCLXXV.

BIBLIOGRAPHY OF HORACE WALPOLE

William Mason to HW, 28 August 1771: 'I am entrusted with all Mr. Gray's papers "to preserve or destroy at my own discretion," an important charge which I shall find myself unable to execute without the advice and assistance of his other friends. . . . Hitherto I have been able to do little more than to sort in parcels the letters of his living friends, that I may return them, or burn them as the parties shall direct me to do. I do not find many of yours.'

HW to Mason, 9 September 1771: 'If he [Gray] has left anything for the press, I flatter myself mine will be allowed to contribute to that office. I shall be very happy to bear all the expense.'

Mason to HW, 21 September 1771: 'After thanking you for the very obliging offer you make of publishing his poems, &c., I will with the same freedom tell you my opinion upon that subject. I always thought Mr. Gray blamable for letting the booksellers have his MSS gratis—I never saw anything myself beneath the dignity of a gentleman in making a profit of the productions of one's own brain. . . . My first business therefore will be to ascertain this right [i.e., whether he or Dodsley controlled the copyright], and afterwards to make as much profit of the book as I possibly can. . . . What I have said does not in the least counteract your thought of an edition from your own press—and I shall be happy to consult you about it when we next meet. I only mean that the edition for public sale shall be contrived to be a lucrative one.'

HW to Mason, 25 September 1771: 'I not only agree with your sentiments, but am flattered that they countenance my own practice. In some cases I have sold my works, and sometimes have made the impressions pay themselves. . . . I am neither ashamed of being an author, nor a bookseller. . . . In short, Sir, I have no notion of poor Mr. Gray's delicacy. . . . I will beg you, Sir, when you come to town to bring me what papers or letters he had preserved of mine.'

Mason to HW, 23 February 1773: 'I have altered my plan of Mr. Gray's life very much. . . . I shall have many occasional notes to insert, which perhaps will be done best as the work goes through the press.'

HW to Mason, 2 March 1773: 'What shall I say? How shall I thank you for the kind manner in which you submit your papers to my correction?'

HW to Mason, 14 December 1773: 'Whenever I have the pleasure of seeing you, we will read over the remainder of the letters [of Gray] together, and burn such as you disapprove of my keeping.'

HW to Mason, 3 April 1775: 'Well! your book is walking the town in midday. How it is liked I do not yet know.'

Quarto; published in London 30 March 1775 by Dodsley, at 15/- in boards. The paper is unwatermarked; an untrimmed copy measures 27.5 x 22 cm. A trimmed copy on large paper, royal quarto, measures 29 x 23 cm.

Signatures: Half-sheet unsigned; A–3F⁴; a–o⁴; one leaf.

Pagination: Fly-title of Memoirs, with verso blank; title-page, with verso blank; [1]–416 Memoirs of Gray; 1–112 Poems and notes;

[113] Errata; [114] blank. The fly-title and title-page are occasionally (and correctly) reversed.

Frontispiece: Portrait of Gray.

Cancels: Kk$_2$ and h$_4$; and leaves Pp$_2$ and Pp$_3$ are a cancel half-sheet.

Mason's letter to HW, 2 October 1774, is of interest: 'I have been occupied of late in filling up those chasms in the Memoirs which the cancelled pages required. I hope I have made them more innocent.'

OTHER EDITIONS

The second edition was published in London early in June, and there was a Dublin edition in 1775. In 1778 a reprint in four volumes, octavo, was published in York. Mason's work was the basis for numerous later editions.

COPIES

1. HW's copy is at Harvard.
2. A copy on large paper, royal quarto, presented by Mason to Norton Nicholls, and bequeathed by Nicholls in 1809 to T. J. Mathias. Diced calf, gilt. Quaritch, January 1937, to WSL, £10.10.0. Since the newspaper advertisements and reviews make no mention of large-paper copies, I assume that there were very few.

59. THE SLEEP-WALKER. 1778.

Prefixed are HW's verses to Lady Craven. For description see the *SH Bibliography*, p. 114.

60. EPILOGUE TO MRS. GRIFFITH'S THE TIMES, A COMEDY. 1780.

The Epilogue is printed in Miss Berry's edition of the *Works*, 1798, iv.402. Presumably her text was printed from HW's MS. The play was acted at Drury Lane, 2 December 1779, and the Epilogue was spoken by HW's friend, Miss Farren, later Countess of Derby.

The text, when it was published in the play in 1780, was very different from the text printed in 1798; only a few lines of the Prologue and a few of the Epilogue, of 1780, are used in the Epilogue as printed in 1798. In HW's notes about the printing of his *Works* (MS at Morgan Library), he listed 'Prologue and Epilogue intended for the comedy of the *Times*'; it seems likely from this note that Miss Berry rejected the texts in the printed play, and used only the Epilogue that she had in HW's autograph. An alternate possibility is that Miss Berry printed from an early draft (it is marked October 1779 in the *Works*), which HW later expanded into the Prologue and Epilogue printed in the play. The text reprinted by WSL, in *HW's Fugitive Verses*, 1931, is that of the *Works*.

THE
TIMES:
A
COMEDY.

AS IT IS NOW PERFORMING AT THE

THEATRE-ROYAL
IN
DRURY-LANE.

By Mrs. GRIFFITH.

LONDON:

Printed for FIELDING and WALKER, Paternoster-Row;
J. DODSLEY, Pall-Mall; T. BECKET, Strand; and
T. DAVIES, Russel-Street, Covent-Garden.

MDCCLXXX.

60.

Octavo in half-sheets; published early in January 1780, at 1/6.
Signatures: Four leaves unsigned; B–L⁴.
Pagination: [i] half-title; [ii] blank; [iii] title-page; [iv] blank; [v]–vi Mrs. Griffith's Advertisement; vii–viii Prologue, Epilogue, and Dramatis Personae; [1]–80 text.

EDITIONS

The play was reprinted in Dublin, in duodecimo, in 1775. The earliest separate printing I have found of the Prologue and Epilogue, as they were printed in the play, is in the *London Chronicle,* 1 January 1780; they were also printed in the *Town and Country Magazine* for December 1779, published early in January.

COPIES

1. HW's copy, presented to him by the author, is in his collection called the *Theatre of George 3,* described in the *SH Bibliography,* p. 257. It is now WSL.

61. RICHARD GOUGH, SEPULCHRAL MONUMENTS. 1786.

Both HW and William Cole contributed a good deal to Gough's antiquarian lore, and there are repeated references to the book in the Yale edition of the *Correspondence with Cole.* As early as 7 February 1782 Cole sent a specimen (proof sheets) of Gough's work to HW. HW lent many drawings, and Gough acknowledged HW's help in his preface and on p. *36.

Cole communicated an extract, from HW's letter to him of 11 August 1769, to Gough, who printed it in his preface. HW was somewhat embarrassed to have his 'hasty indigested sketches' published. See his letter to Gough, 21 June 1786.

Imperial folio; the first part of Volume I was published in June 1786, by Payne, for £6.6.0. (Four additional parts were published in 1796; Lowndes collates the set.)
Signatures (Part I): Two leaves unsigned; A–D²; a–3e²; A¹; B–K²; *K¹; L–T²; U¹; X². Two inserted leaves signed E₂ and I₃.
Pagination: Half-title and title-page, with versos blank; [1]–10 Preface; 11–12 List of plates; 13–14 Contents of the Introduction; fly-title, with quotation on verso; [i]–cxciv Introduction; [cxcv]–cciv Appendix and Table; fly-title, with quotation on verso; 1–36, *35–*36, 37–78 text. Fly-titles (signed E₂ and I₃), with quotations on versos, inserted after pp. 14 and 32.
Plates: Forty-one plates plus engravings in text, as detailed in List of plates.

𝔖𝔢𝔭𝔲𝔩𝔠𝔥𝔯𝔞𝔩 𝔐𝔬𝔫𝔲𝔪𝔢𝔫𝔱𝔰

IN

GREAT BRITAIN

APPLIED TO ILLUSTRATE THE HISTORY OF

FAMILIES, MANNERS, HABITS, AND ARTS,

AT THE DIFFERENT PERIODS

FROM THE NORMAN CONQUEST TO THE SEVENTEENTH CENTURY.

WITH

INTRODUCTORY OBSERVATIONS.

PART I.

CONTAINING THE FOUR FIRST CENTURIES.

La Sculpture peut auffi fournir les Monumens en quantité : *la plupart fur les* TOMBEAUX.
MONTFAUCON.

LONDON,
PRINTED BY J. NICHOLS, FOR THE AUTHOR;
AND SOLD BY T. PAYNE AND SON.
MDCCLXXXVI.

61. REDUCED. WIDTH OF ORIGINAL 21 CM.

Cancels: Since the direction at the end of a sheet is not infrequently wrong, Gough probably revised his text after printing the preceding sheet. The signature is omitted on sheet p, and since the direction on o$_2$ verso is wrong, sheet p is perhaps a revised or cancel sheet.

Copies

Many copies were destroyed by a fire in Nichols's shop, and sets were highly esteemed by the great nineteenth-century collectors; Lowndes records sales of complete sets at prices ranging from £50 to £92. But the Sir Henry Hope Edwardes set now at Farmington, handsomely bound in brown morocco, with presentation inscriptions in first and last parts to James Basire who engraved many of the plates, was purchased by WSL from Sotheran in October 1931 for £9.9.0. HW's set, which was uncut in boards when sold, is unreported since 1842.

62. WALPOLIANA. 1799.

These two small volumes of miscellaneous anecdotes were compiled by John Pinkerton. Although they are only a somewhat poorly arranged 'lounging miscellany,' they include an important biographical sketch of HW and some important miscellaneous information. The anecdotes were first printed serially in the *Monthly Magazine,* published by Richard Phillips, March 1798 to May 1799; and then reprinted in book form, with the biographical sketch of HW, in November 1799. Two volumes, in foolscap octavo, 9/– in boards.

The volumes were printed by Bensley and published by Phillips. Pinkerton suppressed his own name, even from the letters addressed to him by HW. The engraved title-pages read only 'Walpoliana,' with no indication of the compiler. Pinkerton included a folded page containing engraved facsimiles of the writing of Gray and HW.

Editions

A second edition, published in 1800, is a page-for-page reprint. Some years later (the watermark is 1806) this edition was reprinted (by W. Lewis, not by Bensley), using the engraved title-pages marked 'Second Edition.' The second edition is often catalogued as [1804], apparently because Lowndes and Allibone give that date.

An edition was printed in Dublin in January 1800, in one volume duodecimo. The printer made a cheap copy of the engraved title-page for Volume I, but did not attempt the plate of facsimiles.

A miniature edition was published, by John Sharpe, in 1819. This was a companion volume to Sharpe's new edition of HW's *Reminiscences,* published in 1819, and the two are normally bound together. Sharpe printed the Letters at the end of the *Reminiscences,* and re-

WALPOLIANA.

VOL. I.

Mr Gray the poet, has often observed to me, that, if any man were to form a Book of what he had seen and heard himself, it muſt, in whatever hands, prove a moſt uſeful and entertaining one. *Walpole.*

P. Thomson sc.

LONDON.

Printed for R. Phillips, 71, St Paul's Church Yard.

By T. Bensley, Bolt Court, Fleet Street

62.

EDITORIAL CONTRIBUTIONS BY WALPOLE

arranged the anecdotes in *Walpoliana* in alphabetical order. (Another edition was published in 1819 in Sharpe's Select Edition of the British Prose Writers.)

Sharpe's editions of the *Reminiscences* and *Walpoliana* were reprinted in Boston in one volume in 1820; and they were printed by Whittingham in 1830, in his Cabinet Library.

NOTE

Because of the title, it is perhaps proper to record at this point Lord Hardwicke's *Walpoliana*, containing reminiscences of Sir Robert Walpole. This pamphlet was privately printed in February 1781, and revised (with a 'Supplement') in 1783. HW's copy of the edition of 1781, formerly owned by Lord Rosebery, was given by the late Sir Hugh Walpole to the King's School, Canterbury, in 1938. Lord Hardwicke's copy of the edition of 1783 is at Farmington.

63. HENTZNER'S JOURNEY INTO ENGLAND. 1807.

The SH edition of this work, printed in 1758, is properly entered and described in the *SH Bibliography*, p. 31, where this edition is only listed.

The edition of 1807, printed at the private press of T. E. Williams at Reading, is important because it prints for the first time a poem by HW, addressed to Mrs. Porter. It seems to be genuine, even if HW did not collect it in his *Works*.

The editor, Mr. Williams, printed fifty copies by hand, for presents. In his Preface he thanks Francis Annesley, Esq., for his remarks and corrections during the printing; also the Rev. Dr. Valpy, his teacher. 'The SH copy, from which this was taken, is in the possession of Mr. J. Hawthorne; it contains the following complimentary verses addressed by Lord Orford to Mrs. Porter, the celebrated actress, which have never before been printed.'

Francis Annesley was an eager SH Press collector who died in 1812; I do not know who Mr. J. Hawthorne was. The verses may have been written in 1743 when Mrs. Porter retired, or perhaps more probably they were composed in retrospect about 1758, when HW had just printed Hentzner and Mrs. Porter had just distributed Lord Cornbury's *Mistakes*.

Small quarto in half-sheets, printed without signatures.

Pagination: Title-page, with verso blank; one blank leaf; [1]–2 Preface by editor, Mr. Williams; 3 HW's verses to Mrs. Porter; [4] blank; [i]–iii HW's Advertisement, first printed in 1757; [iv] blank; [1]–56 text; [57]–58 Addenda; one blank leaf.

COPIES

The New York Public Library has two copies; one, in contemporary half morocco, has John Trotter Brockett's bookplate.

A JOURNEY INTO ENGLAND.

BY

PAUL HENTZNER,

IN THE YEAR M.D. XC. VIII.

Printed at Strawberry hill, 1757.
Reprinted at the PRIVATE PRESS of T. E. Williams,
READING.
1807

63.

EDITORIAL CONTRIBUTIONS BY WALPOLE

64. THE WORKS OF SIR C. H. WILLIAMS, WITH NOTES BY HORACE WALPOLE. 1822.

HW to Henry Fox, later Lord Holland, 6 February 1760: 'I propose sometime or other with your leave to come to Holland House and write a few notes to his poems [i.e., Williams's]; and I shall in the meantime draw up a little account of him, and will give it you for your manuscript. I need not say to you, that all this will be a secret to everybody else.' In the same letter HW enclosed a proposed epitaph for Williams's monument, a composition that he recorded in his 'Short Notes' and copied in his *Book of Materials*.

The *Works* comprise three volumes, in small octavo, published 29 May 1822, by Edward Jeffery and Son, at £1.11.6. The editor was Jeffery himself.

The notes by HW were printed by Jeffery from the MS notes in Lord Essex's collection at Holland House. Lord Essex was the grandson of Sir Charles Hanbury Williams. The *Dictionary of National Biography* observes that the volumes were 'miserably edited by Jeffery, who on 21 June 1822 had to publish an apology to Lord Essex.' In the British Museum is a copy of Williams's *Collection of Poems*, 1763, with annotations by HW. In the *Waldegrave MS* there are also extensive notes on Williams's life and writings. The MS that HW annotated was still at Holland House in 1947.

65. MEMOIRS OF HORACE WALPOLE AND HIS CONTEMPORARIES. 1851.

The title-page says 'edited by Eliot Warburton,' but his only contribution was a short Introduction. The actual editor or compiler was Robert Folkestone Williams. Although this biography includes little previously unpublished material, it is a somewhat useful gathering of information from HW's letters and from the recollections of many contemporaries.

Two volumes, octavo, published by Henry Colburn, 1851. The set was published at 28/–, but it was reissued in a cheaper edition in 1852 at 16/–.

At Farmington there is an extra-illustrated set bound in four volumes with specially printed title-pages, all dated 1852.

Biographies of HW do not properly come within the scope of this bibliography; but it may be proper to remark here that after the brief 'Biographical Sketch' in Pinkerton's *Walpoliana* in 1799, there was no formal biography of HW until 1851. Of later biographies the most important are perhaps Austin Dobson's, first published in New York in 1890 and (revised by Dr. Toynbee) most recently in 1927; and Mr. R. W. Ketton-Cremer's, in 1940. The longest is that of M. Paul Yvon, in 1924.

Another biography, principally extracts from HW's letters, was published by L. B. Seeley as *Horace Walpole and his World*, 1884.

THE WORKS,

OF THE RIGHT HONOURABLE

SIR CHAS. HANBURY WILLIAMS, K.B.

AMBASSADOR TO THE COURTS OF RUSSIA, SAXONY, &c.

FROM THE ORIGINALS

IN THE POSSESSION OF HIS GRANDSON

THE RIGHT HON. THE EARL OF ESSEX:

WITH NOTES BY

HORACE WALPOLE, EARL OF ORFORD.

IN THREE VOLUMES, WITH PORTRAITS.

VOL. I.

LONDON:
EDWARD JEFFERY AND SON, PALL-MALL.

1822.

64.

MEMOIRS

OF

HORACE WALPOLE

AND

HIS CONTEMPORARIES;

INCLUDING NUMEROUS

ORIGINAL LETTERS CHIEFLY FROM STRAWBERRY HILL.

EDITED BY

ELIOT WARBURTON, Esq.,

AUTHOR OF "THE CRESCENT AND THE CROSS," ETC., ETC.

IN TWO VOLUMES.

VOL. I.

LONDON:
HENRY COLBURN, PUBLISHER,
13, GREAT MARLBOROUGH STREET.
1851.

66. SATIRICAL POEMS PUBLISHED ANONYMOUSLY BY WILLIAM MASON, WITH NOTES BY HORACE WALPOLE. Oxford, 1926.

The editor was Paget Toynbee.

For many years the legend persisted that HW had at least assisted in the composition of Mason's *Heroic Epistle to Sir William Chambers* (1773; several editions from standing type; fifteen editions in three years). In fact, however, he merely assisted in the planned mystification by pretending in letters and conversation that he did not know the author. There is no indication, either, that HW was the author of any part of Mason's *Heroic Postscript* (1774; eight numbered editions printed from standing type).

'Short Notes': 'At the end of May [1779] wrote a commentary and notes to Mr. Mason's later poems.'

The MS from which Dr. Toynbee printed in 1926 was in the Waller Sale in 1921, and is now at Harvard. A first draft in HW's hand, headed 'Notes to Mr. W. Mason's later Poems,' was purchased by WSL in 1937 from Mrs. Richard Bentley, in a collection.

CONTRIBUTIONS TO PERIODICALS, &c.

Gathered here are HW's identified verses and short essays that were first printed in a magazine or newspaper, in order of publication. Omitted are all poems that were first printed in editions of the *Letters* or that were first printed in HW's collected *Works*. I have also omitted all items first printed as Detached Pieces at the SH Press: these are all gathered in the *SH Bibliography*, and it seems needlessly cumbersome to insert a reference for each item as I have for the books printed at the Press.

I have likewise included here publication in anthologies like Dodsley's *Museum* and his *Collection of Poems*, and in modern books.

Pretended advertisement of the She-Witch from Lapland, in *Daily Advertiser*, 28 December 1741.

HW's transcript of this short satirical piece, in the *Waldegrave MS*, includes a note that it was printed in the *Daily Advertiser* for 1742.

Advertisements of monsters of one sort or another are not uncommon in London newspapers: learned horses, unicorns, and giants are crowded among advertisements for lotteries, boxing-matches, and truant apprentices. In the winter of 1741–42, there is a sudden outburst of such freaks: the *Daily Advertiser* has almost none until December 1741, but then for some months it prints two or three to an issue. HW, recently back from Italy, seems to have composed his not particularly ingenious parody after reading of the other freaks.

Essays contributed to *Old England*, 1743–1749.

'Short Notes': '18 June 1743 was printed, in a weekly paper called *Old England, or the Constitutional Journal,* my parody on some scenes of *Macbeth,* called "The Dear Witches." It was a ridicule of the new ministry. . . . 22 October 1743 was published No. 38 of the *Old England Journal,* written by me to ridicule Lord Bath. It was reprinted with three other particular numbers.'

'Short Notes': 'In this year (1747) and the next, and in 1749, I wrote thirteen numbers in a weekly paper, called *Old England, or the Broad-bottom Journal*, but being sent to the printer without a name, they were published horridly deformed and spoiled.'

Old England was a weekly of four pages, folio with horizontal chain-lines. The first number was published 5 February 1743, and it continued (with three changes in title and several changes in its publishing arrangements) until 7 April 1753. The editorship is attributed both to John Banks and William Guthrie.

HW's MSS of five numbers published in 1747, formerly in the Waller Collection, are now WSL.

HW's transcripts of his papers are in the *Waldegrave MS*, and they differ considerably from the printed text. Opposite the first essay he wrote, in 1747, HW explained: 'These papers are here transcribed from the original copies, which were often altered, and sometimes very absurdly, by the editor, to whose want of judgment they were left.' His own printed copies of the two numbers printed in 1743 (18 June and 22 October) are tucked into the *Waldegrave MS*; the number for 18 June, containing 'The Dear Witches' and HW's prefatory letter, is inscribed: 'This belongs to George's Coffee House Temple Barr.'

The reprint of four essays in 1743, which HW recorded in 'Short Notes' for that year, is a small octavo in half-sheets, containing 31 pages. The title reads: *Four letters publish'd in Old England: or, The Constitutional Journal, (Viz. of Oct. the 8th, 22d, 29th, and Nov. the 5th),* London: Printed for B. Cowse, at the Globe in Pater-noster-Row, 1743. It was sold for sixpence.

The fifteen numbers written by HW in 1747–49 (he said 'thirteen' in 'Short Notes') can be identified from his transcripts in the *Waldegrave MS*. They are Nos. 144, 147, 158, 162, 164, 166, 170, 173, 180, 182, 188, 195, 208, 217, 250. They were published 14 February, 7 March, 16 May, 13 and 20 June, 4 July, 1 and 22 August, 10 and 24 October, and 5 December, 1747; 23 January, 23 April, and 25 June, 1748; and 11 February 1749.

Long runs of this very rare journal are at the British Museum, at Farmington, and at Yale.

Speech in Parliament on the Hanoverian troops, 19 January 1744.

HW to Sir Horace Mann, 24 January 1744: 'Last Thursday . . . I was shut up in the House till past ten at night, and the night before till twelve. . . . We carried our own army in Flanders by a majority of 112. Last Wednesday was the great day of expectation: we sat in the committee on the Hanover troops till twelve at night: the numbers were 271 to 226. The next day on the report we sat again till past ten, the opposition having moved to adjourn till Monday, on which we divided 265 to 177. Then the Tories all went away in a body, and the troops were voted.'

In its 'Historical Chronicle' for 19 January, the *Gentleman's Magazine* reports: 'The H——n troops were voted again in the Committee of S——ply, by 45 majority; and on the Report by above 80.'

CONTRIBUTIONS TO PERIODICALS, &c.

Wright, in his edition of HW's *Letters* in 1840, quotes Philip Yorke's *Parliamentary Journal:* 'Young Mr. Walpole's speech met with deserved applause from everybody: it was judicious and elegant.'

A rough draft of HW's speech, on a loose sheet, is among the *Waldegrave MSS.*

The *Gentleman's Magazine* for March 1744 reprinted a supposed extract from HW's speech, with the heading: 'H. Walelop then spoke to the following purpose.' This text is either completely imaginary or a mere fragment, and was probably written by Hawkesworth.

In the *London Magazine* for January 1745, an entirely different speech by HW is printed: this text seems likely to be an accurate reproduction of the substance of the speech, since it resembles HW's rough draft in the *Waldegrave MS.* The same text is reprinted in John Almon's *Debates and Proceedings of the British House of Commons* (1766), i.215–223.

HW's first speech in Parliament, 23 March 1742, is printed with his letter to Horace Mann, 24 March 1742; he himself brands the accounts of that speech in the magazines as wholly false. (See 'Short Notes' and his own note on the letter to Mann.)

Two essays in Dodsley's *Museum*, 1746.

'Short Notes': '12 April 1746 was published, in a magazine called *The Museum,* my "Scheme for a Tax on Message Cards and Notes"; and soon after, "An Advertisement of a pretended new book," which I had written at Florence in 1741.'

In his transcripts of the two essays in *Waldegrave MS*, HW explained the various allusions. HW there says that the 'Advertisement for a History of Good Breeding' was written in 1740, but his dates are not always entirely accurate and he was in Florence through much of 1740 and until the spring of 1741. For publication in 1746, he revised his MS copy somewhat.

The Museum: or, The literary and historical register was published twice a month by Dodsley. It was continued through thirty-nine numbers, from March 1746 to September 1747. Each number contained five half-sheets, in octavo. HW's two essays are in the second and fifth numbers; the editor's note says that the first one 'was designed to have been inserted in the First Number, but came too late.' The editor was Mark Akenside.

Both essays were reprinted in *Fugitive Pieces,* 1758, and in the quarto *Works* of 1770 and 1798.

'Verses occasion'd by a Late Will,' in *London Evening Post,* No. 2908, 26 June 1746.

The will in question was that of John Spencer, Esq., who died 19 June 1746. See HW to Montagu, 24 June 1746: 'The great business of the town, is Jack Spencer's will, who has left Althrop and the Sunderland estate in reversion to

Pitt, after more obligations and more pretended friendship for his brother the Duke than is conceivable. . . .'

The *London Evening Post,* 24 June 1746, reported: 'We hear that John Spencer, Esq., lately deceased, has devised the Reversion of his Estate, unintail'd, in case his Son should die without issue, to his four Executors, *viz.* Lord Chesterfield, Mr. Pitt, Dr. Stevens, and Lord Fane.'

HW's transcript of the verses (with two other fragments) is in the *Waldegrave MS,* and a copy he clipped from the newspaper is in Lord Waldegrave's collection. The verses themselves are sufficiently undistinguished, twenty-three lines in heroic couplets (one triplet).

The *London Evening Post* was published three times a week, in folio. The set at the University of Illinois includes the number for 26 June 1746. Another set is in the Burney Collection at the British Museum.

'An Epistle from Florence to Thomas Ashton, Esq.' in Dodsley's *Collection of Poems,* January 1748, ii.305.

This poem was written early in 1740. The text that HW transcribed in *Waldegrave MS* differs considerably from the text Dodsley printed; since in two lines the text of the *Waldegrave MS* was corrected after the Dodsley text had been copied in, it seems possible that the whole *Waldegrave MS* text is later. But this is somewhat speculative: it is just as possible that the text was copied in the *Waldegrave MS* first (as one would expect), then an extensively revised copy was given to Dodsley in 1748, and finally at some later time two corrections were made in the *Waldegrave MS.* Or, if these two corrections were made before 1748, HW forgot about them when he revised another copy for Dodsley. The text used in Dodsley is that used in HW's *Fugitive Pieces* of 1758, and in the *Works* of 1770 and 1798. The poem was also reprinted in the first volume of Bell's *Fugitive Poetry* in 1789.

Also included in Dodsley's *Collection,* just after the 'Epistle from Florence,' were reprints of 'The Beauties' and the 'Epilogue to Tamerlane,' at the end of the second volume.

A complete bibliography of Dodsley's famous *Collection* is not needed here; a full description can be found in Arthur Case's *Bibliography of English Poetical Miscellanies.* HW sent a set of the first edition to Gray, who objected to the title vignette (the three Graces unclothed) and to the cheap paper and poor typography. (*Correspondence of Gray,* ed. Toynbee and Whibley, 1935, i.294.) The Graces were removed from the second edition.

Full details of the writing and printing of the 'Epistle from Florence' may be found in *HW's Fugitive Verses.*

Essays in *The Remembrancer,* 1748-49.

'Short Notes': 'I next wrote [1748] two papers of the *Remembrancer,* and two more of the same in the year 1749.'

CONTRIBUTIONS TO PERIODICALS, &c.

The *Remembrancer,* a weekly paper somewhat in the manner of the *Spectator,* was published from December 1747 to June 1751. The editor was James Ralph. From June to November, 1753, Ralph published a kind of sequel, the *Protester,* in twenty-four numbers.

HW's transcripts of his essays in the *Remembrancer* are in the *Waldegrave MS.* He wrote No. 32 (16 July 1748), No. 38 (27 August 1748), No. 97 (14 October 1749), and a fourth number that was not printed.

Essays in *The World,* 1753.

'Short Notes': '8 February 1753, was published a paper I had written in a periodical work, called the *World,* published by E. Moore. I wrote eight more numbers, besides two that were not printed then; and one containing a character of Mr. Fox, which I had written some years before.' HW actually contributed not 'eight more numbers,' but eight in all besides the character of Fox.

To many people the *World* is perhaps best known as the magazine in which, in 1754, Chesterfield published his bid for a reconciliation with Samuel Johnson just before the *Dictionary* was published. It was published from 4 January 1753 to 30 December 1756. The principal undertaker was Edward Moore under the name of Adam Fitz-Adam.

HW's contributions, identified from his transcripts in the *Waldegrave MS,* are as follows:

No. 6, Thursday, 8 February 1753
8, Thursday, 22 February 1753
10, Thursday, 8 March 1753
14, Thursday, 5 April 1753
28, Thursday, 12 July 1753, 'written at Strawberry Hill'
103, Thursday, 19 December 1754, 'written at Strawberry Hill'
160, Thursday, 22 January 1756, 'written at Strawberry Hill'
195, Thursday, 23 September 1756, 'written at Chaffont Place'

'A World Extraordinary,' published in January 1757 just after the last regular number of the *World,* containing the character of Fox. The MS copy is marked 'Strawberry Hill 1748,' but it was somewhat revised for publication. The copy he sent to Lady Caroline Fox in 1748 was in the Waller Collection.

Now at Farmington also are the MSS of two unpublished *Worlds,* no doubt written at about the same time but not used; likewise two others that were first published in *Fugitive Pieces* in 1758, and reprinted in the *London Magazine* for September, 1784. These MSS seem to have been among the papers acquired by Richard Bentley from Miss Berry, and they were bought by WSL from the present Mrs. Bentley.

Each number of the *World* was a sheet and a half, pot folio. The agreement between Dodsley and Moore mentions that the paper is to be 'one sheet and a half printed in the manner of the *Rambler,*' and the *World* does resemble the

Rambler in paper and typography. (The agreement is reprinted in R. Straus, *Robert Dodsley*, p. 186.)

Bound sets of the *World* are perhaps about as rare as sets of the *Rambler*. HW's own untrimmed printed copies of the numbers he wrote, revised and annotated for inclusion in his *Fugitive Pieces* of 1758, are now at Farmington. HW's most interesting changes are the insertions of all the passages deleted from his essays by the editor in 1753; these passages are also marked in his transcripts in *Waldegrave MS*.

Like the *Rambler*, the *World* was reprinted at once in duodecimo, and in that format there were a half-dozen editions before 1800. HW's set of the first collected edition in six volumes (1755–57), probably SH Sale, vi.18, is now in the Morgan Library: it is bound in original calf, rebacked, with HW's bookplate and some annotations by him. HW indicated the authorship of each number when it was known to him, and indexed the names at the end of each volume. On the title-page of the first volume he marked the motto from Ovid as chosen by him, and added that he had also chosen the motto for the folio edition.

HW's essays were reprinted in his *Fugitive Pieces* of 1758, and in his *Works* of 1770 and 1798.

Essay contributed to James Ralph's *Protester*, No. 23, 3 November 1753.

The *Protester* continued for twenty-four numbers in folio, from June to November 1753. It was a weekly essay, somewhat in the manner of the *Spectator* and of Ralph's *Remembrancer*. Ralph's pseudonym was Issachar Barebone.

HW's transcript of his essay is in the *Waldegrave MS*; to it he added the following note: 'This was a weekly paper written by Ralph, and supported at the expense of the Duke of Bedford and Alderman Beckford. There was but one number printed after this [HW's No. 23], Ralph being bought off by the Court. The occasion of this paper was a letter sent by the Earl of Holdernesse, one of the Secretaries of State, to the Chancellor of Ireland, in answer to a memorial which had been presented to the King by the Earl of Kildare, against the Primate of that island.'

'Strawberry-Hill, a Ballad,' in the *Gentleman's Magazine*, April 1756.

William Pulteney, Earl of Bath, wrote two stanzas of the ballad; HW sent these to Bentley, 17 July 1755: 'My Lord Bath . . . has made the following stanzas, to the old tune which you remember of Rowe's ballad on Dodington's Mrs. Strawbridge. . . . Can there be an odder revolution of things, than that the printer of the *Craftsman* [Richard Francklin] should live in a house of mine, and that the author of the *Craftsman* should write a panegyric on a house of mine?' On the same day HW sent the stanzas to George Montagu.

HW added three more stanzas to the ballad as it was printed. Its first printing seems to have been in the *Gentleman's Magazine*. See HW to Montagu, 19 May 1756: 'Pray tell me in what magazine is the Strawberry-ballad.'

A somewhat altered text was printed in the *London Chronicle*, 10 August 1758. Pulteney's stanzas are the first and third, and the fourth stanza of the text in the *Gentleman's Magazine* has been placed second. The wording is also slightly revised. This revised text was reprinted in the *Description of SH*, in 1774 and 1784; in the *New Foundling Hospital for Wit*, in 1784; in the *Works* of 1798; and in *HW's Fugitive Verses*, 1931.

A separate ballad-printing on cheap paper is preserved in Richard Bull's collection of SH pieces, now in the Huntington Library. The text is so close to that printed in the *London Chronicle* that it must have been the source of the *Chronicle's* text, or else printed from the *Chronicle*. I have little doubt that it was printed about 1758, but not at SH. At Farmington there is preserved an engraved copy with music 'set by Mr. Vernon' [i.e., Joseph Vernon]; the text was perhaps derived from oral tradition, since it has most features of the text printed in the *London Chronicle* but follows the text of the *Gentleman's Magazine* in two places. Another engraved copy with the music, p. 54 of an unidentified volume of songs, is at Farmington in a miscellaneous collection; the text is close to that printed in the *London Chronicle*.

In H. Howard's *Choice Spirits Museum, A Collection of Songs*, 1765, there is a parody of 'Strawberry-Hill' called 'The Hills of London,' apparently written about 1758.

Verses to General Conway, in the *Public Advertiser*, 28 November 1757.

HW to General Conway, November 1757: 'In the meantime I send you a most hasty performance.... The Lord knows if it is not sad stuff. I wish for the sake of the subject it were better!' The letter with the MS of the poem is now in the Morgan Library.

HW to Grosvenor Bedford, Saturday, [26 November 1757]: 'I beg you will get the enclosed stanzas inserted in the *Public Advertiser* on Monday next, just as I have written them. If not in the *Public*, then in the *Daily Advertiser*. My name must not be mentioned, nor anything but the initial letters H. C.'

The twenty lines, beginning 'When Fontenoy's impurpled plain,' were printed correctly enough. They have been reprinted frequently in collections of the letters, and in *HW's Fugitive Verses*, 1931. Both Cunningham and Mrs. Toynbee misprinted HW's 'Thou' in the last line as 'Then.'

Political papers in the *London Evening Post*, 1764.

John Almon, in his *Biographical, Literary, and Political Anecdotes*, 1797, i.65, says that in 1764 HW wrote a few political papers in the *London Evening Post*; and in 1766, a few in the *Public Advertiser*.

It is my guess that 1766 is Almon's error for 1767, when HW identifies in his

'Short Notes' two letters to the *Public Advertiser*. It is perhaps likely enough that HW sent some letters to the *London Evening Post* in 1764; but they have so far escaped detection, and I have no ready access to a file. If I had access to the *London Evening Post*, I should hope to find a paragraph attacking the Duke of Bedford as leader of the plan to abolish vails. In his *Memoirs of George III*, 1845, ii.3, HW says: 'As one of my objects was to raise the characters and popularity of our party, I had inserted a paragraph in the newspapers observing that the abolition of vails to servants had been set on foot by the Duke of Bedford, and had been opposed and not complied with by the Duke of Devonshire and family of Cavendish. Soon after, a riot happened at Ranelagh, in which the footmen mobbed and ill-treated some gentlemen who had been active in that reformation.' HW's letter must have been written after the dismissal of General Conway, 21 April 1764, and before the Ranelagh riot on 4 May.

Letter from the King of Prussia to Rousseau, in *St. James's Chronicle*, 3 April 1766.

The trifling joke that HW showed to his friends produced a quarrel far out of proportion to its merit, and the *Cambridge Bibliography* has to allot a special sub-section to Hume's quarrel with Rousseau. The quotations selected herewith present only the Walpolian part of the quarrel.

'Short Notes': 'End of this year [1765, in Paris] wrote the Letter from the King of Prussia to Rousseau. . . . 20 August 1767. I went to Paris. Wrote there an account of my whole concern in the affair of Rousseau, not with intention to publish it yet.' HW's account, as he wrote it in September 1767, is printed in the *Works* of 1798, iv.247–269.

HW to Conway, 12 January 1766: 'My present fame is owing to a very trifling composition. . . . I was one evening at Madame Geoffrin's joking on Rousseau's affectations and contradictions, and said some things that diverted them. When I came home, I put them into a letter, and showed it next day to Helvétius and the Duc de Nivernois; who were so pleased with it, that, after telling me some faults in the language, which you may be sure there were, they encouraged me to let it be seen. . . . I was not averse. The copies have spread like wildfire. . . . Here is the letter. . . . You will say I am a bold man to attack both Voltaire and Rousseau. It is true; but I shoot at their heel, at their vulnerable part.'

HW to Chute, 15 January 1766: 'I enclose a trifle that I wrote lately, which got about and has made enormous noise in a city where they run and cackle after an event, like a parcel of hens after an accidental husk of a grape. It has made me the fashion, and made Madame de Boufflers and the Prince of Conti [Rousseau's protectors] very angry with me. . . .'

HW to Cole, 18 January 1766: 'Rousseau is gone to England with Mr. Hume. You will probably see a letter to Rousseau, in the name of the King of Prussia, writ to laugh at his affectations. It has made excessive noise here, and I believe quite ruined the author with many of the philosophers. When I tell you I was the author, it is telling you how cheap I hold their anger. If it does not reach you, you shall see it at Strawberry.' Cole was impatient to see it, and HW therefore sent him a transcript of it, 25 February 1766.

HW to Miss Anne Pitt, 19 January 1766: 'Would you believe it, Madam, that I am the fashion? . . . An unlucky letter which I wrote in the name of the King of Prussia to Rousseau got about. . . . Everybody would have a copy; the next thing was, everybody would see the author. Thus was I dandled about, with my little arms and legs shaking like a *pantin*. . . . I thought at last I should have a box quilted for me like Gulliver, be set upon the dressing-table of a Maid of Honor, and fed with bonbons. . . . Here is the unfortunate letter. . . .'

After sending copies of his little hoax to so many people, HW could not have been especially astonished when it was published in the *St. James's Chronicle,* in April. Rousseau had gone to England in January, at Hume's invitation and almost as his guest, and to his excitable imagination the letter seemed an insult either planned or permitted by Hume. Rousseau wrote a hurt reply dated 7 April which was published in the *St. James's Chronicle,* 10 April 1766. The editor appended a note saying that the letter to Rousseau had been planned only as a joke, that it had been handed around in MS for weeks, and that its author was well known in *The Catalogue of Noble Authors.*

HW to Mann, 11 July 1766: 'Rousseau has answered all I thought and said of him, by a most weak and passionate answer to my letter, which showed I had touched his true sore.'

HW wrote to Hume, 26 July 1766, to explain his own position. But Hume prepared an account of the whole quarrel, including the letter that helped to start the quarrel and HW's letter of 26 July. This account was translated into French by J.-B. Suard, *Exposé succinct de la contestation entre M. Hume et M. Rousseau,* and published at Paris in the autumn; it was advertised as 'just imported' into England, 8 November 1766; retranslated into English, *A concise and genuine account of the dispute between Mr. Hume and Mr. Rousseau,* and published by Becket, 20 November; translated into Italian in 1767. *A Defense of Mr. Rousseau,* with a severe dedicatory letter to HW, was published by Bladon in November 1766; it is attributed to Edward Burnaby Greene.

HW to Duchesse d'Aiguillon, 3 November 1766: 'Mr. Hume has, I own, surprised me, by suffering his squabble with Rousseau to be published. . . . For my own part, I little expected to see my letter in print, as your Grace tells me it is, for I have not yet seen the book. [He acquired a copy of the English translation soon afterwards; it is in the sixteenth volume of his *Collection of Tracts,* now WSL.] I have neither been asked nor given any consent to my letter being published. I do not take it ill of Mr. Hume, as I left him at liberty to show it to whom he pleased; I am, however, sorry it is printed. . . . I think all literary controversies ridiculous, impertinent, and contemptible. . . . I don't know who the publishers are, nor care. . . . I am told it is asserted that I have owned that the letter to Rousseau was not mine; I wish it was not, for then it would have been better. I told your Grace, I believe, what I told to many more, that some grammatical faults in it had been corrected for me. . . . The book too, I hear, says that the real author ought to discover himself. I was the real author, and never denied it. . . .'

HW wrote two more letters to Hume about the matter, 6 and 11 November 1766. His part in the famous quarrel may perhaps be counted as ended by the publication of Ralph Heathcote's *Letter to the Honorable Mr. Horace Walpole concerning the dispute between Hume and Rousseau*, 9 December 1766. (HW's copy is now at Farmington.)

Hume's part in the quarrel may be traced in detail in his *Letters* (ed. J. Y. T. Greig, 1932); Hume attempted to deposit all his papers dealing with the quarrel in the British Museum, but the Trustees of the Museum did not think proper to receive them, and the papers are therefore with the Hume MSS in the Royal Society of Edinburgh.

Letter to the Mayor of Lynn, in *St. James's Chronicle*, 28 May 1767.

'Short Notes': 'March [1767]. Wrote to the Mayor of Lynn, that I did not intend to come into Parliament again. . . . May 28th. My letter to the Mayor of Lynn was first published in the *St. James's Chronicle*.'

'Short Notes,' at end of 1768: 'I should have mentioned that on the dissolution of the Parliament this year, I refused to serve again, agreeably to a letter I had written to the Mayor of Lynn, and which was published in the newspapers.'

For Wiart's translation into French, see Madame du Deffand's letter to HW, 6 June 1767; his MS is now wsl, together with the transcript of the English original (containing small corrections by HW) that HW sent to Madame du Deffand.

The letter to the Mayor, William Langley, dated 13 March 1767, was reprinted in the *Gentleman's Magazine* for June 1767; and in J. Almon's *Biographical, Literary, and Political Anecdotes*, 1797, i.65. It was first collected in HW's correspondence by Cunningham. In the British Museum is a single-sheet folio printed copy of the letter, possibly but I think probably not an earlier printing than that in the *St. James's Chronicle*.

HW sat as Member for King's Lynn in Norfolk from 1757 to 1768. He was succeeded in 1768 by his cousin, Thomas Walpole, whose letter to the voters, dated 18 March 1767 (doubtless written after consultation with HW and with Lord Orford), was printed in the *St. James's Chronicle* for 21 March 1767. On 19 March 1767 Charles Townshend wrote to Philip Case of Lynn about Thomas Walpole's candidacy. (See the letter printed by H. L. Bradfer-Lawrence in the *Supplement to Blomefield's Norfolk*, 1929.)

Two letters in the *Public Advertiser*, 1767.

'Short Notes': 'In September were published, in the *Public Advertiser*, two letters I had written on political abuse in newspapers. They were signed, *Toby*, and *A Constant Correspondent*.'

CONTRIBUTIONS TO PERIODICALS, &c.

The first letter, signed 'Toby,' was printed 28 August 1767. The second letter, which professes to be a response from a hack writer to Toby's letter, was printed 2 September 1767.

The MSS of both letters are now at Farmington, purchased by WSL in 1937 from Mrs. Richard Bentley, in a collection of Walpolian MSS.

'To the Authoress of some lines on Strawberry-Hill,' in Mendez's *Collection of the most esteemed Pieces of Poetry*, 1767.

The 'Authoress' is identified by Mendez as 'Miss M——,' i.e., Jael Mendez; her married name was Mrs. J. Henrietta Pye (Mrs. Robert Hampden Pye). She died in 1782. Her *Poems*, privately printed in 1767, contain HW's verses on p. 11, possibly an earlier printing than that in the anthology. The episode that produced HW's poem is described by HW in his letter to Cole, 25 April 1775. The verses are reprinted in *HW's Fugitive Verses*, 1931, p. 186.

HW's copy of the *Poems*, presented by the authoress, was in SH Sale, vi.33; resold at Sotheby's, 23 March 1868 (B. G. Windus Sale), lot 744.

'Epilogue spoken by Mrs. Clive,' in *Public Advertiser*, 24 April 1769.

'Short Notes': '24 April 1769. Mrs. Clive spoke an epilogue I had written for her on quitting the stage.'

The epilogue was also printed in the *St. James's Chronicle*, 25 April 1769, and other papers; in the *Town and Country Magazine*, April 1769; in the *Gentleman's Magazine*, May 1769; in the *Annual Register* for 1769; in the *Works* of 1798; and in *HW's Fugitive Verses*, 1931.

Lines on the Duchess of Queensberry, in the *Gentleman's Magazine*, March 1772.

HW to Mann, 26 April 1771: 'The Duchess of Queensberry, a much older veteran, is still figuring in the world. . . . Reflect, that she was a goddess in Prior's days. I could not help adding these lines on her—you know his end:

> Kitty, at heart's desire,
> Obtained the chariot for a day,
> And set the world on fire.

This was some fifty-six years ago, or more. I gave her this stanza: "To many a Kitty. . . ." And she is old enough to be pleased with the compliment.'

The verses (a quatrain) are reprinted in the *Annual Register* for 1772; in the *Fugitive Miscellany*, 1774; in the *Public Advertiser* for 30 August 1780; in the *New Foundling Hospital for Wit*, 1784; in the *Works* of 1798; and in *HW's Fugitive Verses*, 1931.

Verses for the monument to Queen Catherine at Ampthill, in the *Public Advertiser*, 19 October 1773.

In a letter to Cole, 12 October 1771, HW sent a copy of his verses, explaining that he designed them for the monument that Lord Ossory was planning to erect. James Essex designed the monument, but HW's letter to Cole, 22 June 1771, shows that he himself initiated the whole scheme.

In 1773 the monument was completed, and the *Public Advertiser* appears to have published HW's verses as an item of news about the completion of the monument.

A MS copy of the verses by Thomas Kirgate is in his copy of HW's *Fugitive Pieces*, 1758, now WSL.

The verses were reprinted in the *London Magazine* for October 1773; in the first volume of the *New Foundling Hospital for Wit*, 1784; in Richard Gough's edition of Camden's *Britannia*, 1789; and frequently in the nineteenth century.

HW's draft of these verses is in his *Book of Materials*, 1771, now in the Folger Library; there also are 'Verses for an Urn designed to be erected by Lord Ossory at Ampthill to the memory of his cousin the Marquis of Tavistock,' I think never published.

'The Three Vernons,' in the *St. James's Chronicle*, 17 November 1787.

'Short Notes': 'In July [1774] wrote the verses on *The Three Vernons*.' HW must have sent them to Lady Ossory almost immediately, but he planned to keep them secret from most of his friends. In his letter to Lady Ossory, 11 August 1774, he tells an amusing anecdote of his embarrassment at showing them to Richard Owen Cambridge.

The verses were reprinted more correctly in the *Gentleman's Magazine* for November 1787, in the *Annual Register* for 1787, and again in the third volume of the *Asylum for Fugitive Pieces*, 1789. It was perhaps this latter printing, more inaccurate than the others, that HW referred to in his letter to Lady Ossory, 4 August 1789. This poorer text was reprinted in the *Universal Magazine* for August 1789. The verses were included in the fourth volume of the *Works* of 1798, and in *HW's Fugitive Verses*, 1931.

Epitaph on Mrs. Clive's monument in Twickenham Church, in *London Evening Post*, 22 September 1791.

HW's printer, Thomas Kirgate, preserved a clipping of this epitaph, in his copy of the *Description of SH* (1784) now WSL. He marked the first ten lines 'By Miss Pope' and the last six 'By Mr. H. Walpole.' Since HW succeeded to the Earldom in December of 1791, Kirgate must have marked the clipping when it was published. There seems no need to reject Kirgate's evidence.

For HW's earlier pretended epitaph on Mrs. Clive, written in 1774, see the *SH Bibliography*, p. 237.

CONTRIBUTIONS TO PERIODICALS, &c.

'To Edward Jerningham,' in the *European Magazine,* XXVIII (1795), 47.

These lines were occasioned by hearing Jerningham read his new comedy, *The Welch Heiress,* played at Drury Lane 17 April 1795. The eight lines, beginning 'The Nymphs of Pindus have in various ways,' are signed 'Orford.' The note in the *European Magazine* says: 'The following lines, written by the Literary Nestor, Lord Orford, display a sprightliness that seldom accompanies so advanced a time of life.'

In Richard Bull's collection of SH Detached Pieces at the Huntington Library there is a MS copy of the verses, sent to Bull by the bookseller Clarke of Bond Street.

A new number of *The Spectator,* 1772. HW's heading is: 'The Spectator. No. none. written by nobody.' Sunday, 19 January 1772.

HW's rough draft is in the Berry Papers, in the British Museum's Additional MS 37728. He sent a clean copy to Lady Ossory, and it was published in 1848 by R. Vernon Smith with the *Letters Addressed to the Countess of Ossory;* this MS is still with the Ossory papers in private hands.

Also published with the *Letters to the Countess of Ossory* in 1848 were: 'The Peach in Brandy,' written in December 1771 and printed as one of his *Hieroglyphic Tales* in 1785; and a short 'Sequel to *Gulliver's Travels,'* also written in December 1771.

'The Garland,' in the *Quarterly Review,* March 1852.

'Short Notes': 'July 16 [1761], wrote *The Garland,* a poem on the King, and sent it to Lady Bute, but not in my own hand, nor with my name, nor did I ever own it.'

HW to Grosvenor Bedford, Sunday, [19 July 1761]: 'I will beg you to copy the following lines for me, and bring or send them, whichever is most convenient to you, to my house in Arlington Street on Tuesday morning. Pray don't mention them to anybody.'

The verses were reprinted in Cunningham's edition of the *Letters,* and Mrs. Toynbee's; and in *HW's Fugitive Verses,* 1931.

'Memoir of Gray,' in *The Correspondence of Gray and Mason,* 1853.

This volume was edited by the Rev. John Mitford. A more correct text was published by Paget Toynbee in the *Modern Language Review,* 1932, and reprinted as Appendix Y in *The Correspondence of Thomas Gray,* ed. Toynbee and Whibley, 1935; this corrected text was printed from HW's transcript in the *Waldegrave MS.*

It may be assumed that HW wrote his 'Memoir' soon after Gray's death.

BIBLIOGRAPHY OF HORACE WALPOLE

'Verses to My Pen,' written to Miss Berry about 1793.

These lines were published by Lady Theresa Lewis in the first volume of the *Journals and Correspondence of Miss Berry*, 1865, p. 429.

Chanson on Lady Caroline Petersham and Col. Conway.

These verses, in French and English, written probably about 1744, were printed in the Eighth Report of the Historical MSS Commission, 1881; and reprinted in Appendix 1 of the Yale edition of HW's *Correspondence with George Montagu*, 1941.

'Seeds of Poetry and Rhime,' written in 1736.

These verses were printed by Gosse in his edition of Gray's *Works* (1884), i.205, and attributed to Gray because of a transcript at Pembroke College in his autograph. But the transcript by Gray is signed with what is now known to be HW's *nom de plume*.

The verses were printed from HW's autograph, in a letter to West, in Toynbee's *Correspondence of Gray, Walpole, West, and Ashton* (1915), i.118. They were reprinted in *HW's Fugitive Verses*, 1931. The original letter is now WSL.

Mock Sermon to Lady Mary Coke, printed in the third volume of *The Letters and Journals of Lady Mary Coke*, Edinburgh 1892.

'Short Notes': 'May 30th [1761], wrote a mock sermon to dissuade Lady Mary Coke from going to the King's birthday, as she had lately been ill.'

Also included in the same volume of Lady Mary's *Letters and Journals* are HW's lines to Mrs. Pitt, 'To raise a troop a thousand ask'; and a facsimile of the verses to Lady Mary printed with HW's letter to Montagu, 23 December 1761.

'Journals of Visits to Country Seats,' 1751–1784.

These notes are in HW's *Books of Materials*, now in the Folger Library. They were published by Dr. Paget Toynbee in the sixteenth volume of the Walpole Society, 1927–28.

'Delenda est Oxonia,' a political pamphlet, written in 1749.

First published by Dr. Paget Toynbee from the *Waldegrave MS* in the *English Historical Review*, XLII (1927), 95–108.

'Walpoliana,' transcribed by Dr. Paget Toynbee from HW's *Books of Materials* and *Paris Journals*.

These selections were first published by Dr. Toynbee in *Blackwood's Maga-*

zine, CCXXI (1927), 454–463. The *Paris Journals* were published completely in the fifth volume of the Yale edition of HW's *Correspondence with Mme. du Deffand* (1939).

The originals, formerly in the collection of Sir Wathen Waller, are now in the Folger Library (*Books of Materials*) and in the Merritt Collection at Harvard (*Paris Journals*).

'Notes on the Exhibitions of the Society of Artists and the Free Society, 1760–1791.'

These notes were printed, from HW's set of the catalogues now at Farmington, in the twenty-seventh volume of the Walpole Society, 1938–39. They were transcribed and edited by Mr. Hugh Gatty.

BOOKS DEDICATED TO WALPOLE

This list is not precisely part of HW's bibliography, but since its only unity comes from HW, it may provide an interesting appendage to the bibliography. The list may not be complete; I record as briefly as possible the books I have gathered. Seven miscellaneous pieces are appended.

[Blizard, Sir William]. 'Stanzas on viewing Strawberry-Hill: inscribed to the Right Honourable Horace Walpole, Earl of Orford.' Privately printed; dated 18 August 1793. A transcript in Kirgate's hand is preserved in HW's extra-illustrated *Description of SH*.

Carter, John. *Specimens of Ancient Sculpture and Painting*, folio, 1780.

Craven, Elizabeth Berkeley, Lady (later Margravine of Anspach). *A Modern Anecdote*, 1779. The story was dramatized in 1781 by Miles Peter Andrews.

Felton, Samuel. *Imperfect Hints towards a new edition of Shakespeare*, 1787–88. (Dedicated to HW and Sir Joshua Reynolds.)

Gilpin, William. *Essay on Prints*, 3d ed., 1781; also 4th ed., 1792. The dedication copy of the edition of 1781, with HW's bookplate and notes, was sold at Sotheby's, 23 March 1868 (B. G. Windus Sale), lot 352; Dr. Dibdin bought it at the SH Sale. It was later owned by Lady Dorothy Nevill and is now at Farmington.

Granger, James. *Biographical Dictionary*, 1769. See the full description in the bibliography above, pp. 130–35.

Ives, John. *Select Papers*, 1773.

Jephson, Robert. *The Count of Narbonne*, 1781. HW's copy of the Dublin reprint of 1782 is owned by Mrs. Scott-Murray of Heckfield Place, bound with the *Castle of Otranto*, 1782.

Jerningham, Edward. *The Swedish Curate*, 1773.

Knight, E. Cornelia. *Marcus Flaminius*. Two volumes, octavo, 1792.

Lysons, Daniel. *The Environs of London*, 1792. HW's set is now at Farmington.

More, Hannah. *Florio*, 1786.

[169]

BIBLIOGRAPHY OF HORACE WALPOLE

Patch, Thomas. *Life of Fra Bartolommeo*, [Florence] 1772.

Pinkerton, John. *Essay on Medals*, 2d ed., 1789. HW declined the dedication of the first edition; see his letter to James Dodsley, 8 August 1784. The dedication copy of the edition of 1789 is now in the British Museum.

Whaley, John. *A Collection of original Poems and Translations*, 1745. One poem, 'In Imitation of Horace' on p. 83, was especially addressed to HW; the MS of this poem was sold with Whaley's letters in the Waller Collection in 1921. William Cole, in his *Paris Journal of 1765*, pp. 65, 73–80, gives his recollections of Whaley. Cole's copy of the *Poems* of 1745 is now in the British Museum. HW's copy is in the Dyce Collection.

[?Whaley, John]. *The Miser*, a poem: from the first satire of the first book of Horace, 1735.

The World, 1755. The second volume of the duodecimo edition was dedicated to HW.

In January 1764 Alexander Bannerman (who engraved a number of the portraits in the *Anecdotes of Painting*) dedicated to HW an engraving of the cave scene in *Macbeth*, from the painting by P. Dawe.

Burrell, Lady. *Lines sent to Mr. Walpole by an anonymous author in 1790*. Privately printed by Richard Bull, 1791.

'On Seeing Strawberry-Hill, the Seat of Horace Walpole, Esq.' Verses in *Gentleman's Magazine*, April 1778, signed 'Y.' A transcript in Kirgate's hand is preserved in HW's extra-illustrated *Description of SH*.

'A Retreat for the Gods, a poem, inscribed to the elegant genius of Strawberry Hill.' Verses in the *Morning Post*, 24 August 1780.

The Genuine Copy of a Letter found, Nov. 5, 1782, near Strawberry-Hill, Twickenham. Addressed to the Hon. Mr. H——ce W——le, 1783. (On the quarrel with Chatterton.)

Moody, Elizabeth. 'On the death of Horace Walpole, Earl of Orford,' published in her *Poetical Trifles*, 1798.

[Wolcot, John]. Verses addressed to Walpole on his epitaph on Mrs. Clive, in *Public Advertiser*, 14 October 1791; frequently reprinted. See *HW's Fugitive Verses*, p. 87.

APOCRYPHA

Listed herewith are numerous items that have for one reason or another been incorrectly ascribed to HW, with the briefest possible notes of identification.

1. *The Medalist,* a six-penny ballad published by Huggonson in December 1741, is attributed doubtfully to HW in Halkett and Laing's *Dictionary* and in Stonehill and Block's *Anonyma and Pseudonyma.* There are copies at the British Museum, Harvard, the Huntington Library, and the University of Cincinnati. It is a satire on Sir Robert Walpole's administration, and so can hardly be by HW.

2. *A Proclamation, a poem,* published by Webb in 1750, has been attributed to HW by two major American libraries. The mistake seems to arise from a misunderstanding of the British Museum's *Catalogue,* where a copy is recorded as having 'MS Notes [by Horace Walpole].'

3. Robert Whytt's *Essay on the Virtues of Lime-water in the Cure of the Stone,* Edinburgh 1752 and later editions, is often catalogued under Walpole because of an appendix containing an account of the case of the Hon. Horatio Walpole written by himself. The account, published originally in the Royal Society's *Philosophical Transactions* for 1751, is by HW's uncle, Horatio Walpole, 1st Baron Walpole.

4. *An Essay on the Liberty of the Press,* Raymond, 1754, is attributed to HW by Isaac Reed (in a MS note) and by Lowndes. But HW inscribed his own copy, 'By the Archdeacon of Norwich,' i.e., Thomas Hayter. An entirely different 'Dissertation on the Liberty of the Press' was printed serially in *Old England,* 1747–48, but this cannot be by HW, either.

5. *Considerations on the present German War,* 1760. This pamphlet, mentioned by Lowndes under HW, was written by Israel Mauduit.

6. *A Vindication of the Conduct of the Present War,* Tonson, 1760, is attributed to HW by Isaac Reed (in a MS note) because it was published by Tonson; and the attribution is accepted by Lowndes. But it is dated Berkshire, 15 December 1760, when HW was in London; and HW made no annotation on his own copy, now WSL, although he identified the authors of three other pamphlets bound with it. The fact of publication by Tonson seems not significant to me: Reed thought HW used Tonson (by way of Grosvenor Bedford)

for pamphlets he did not wish to acknowledge. (The *Vindication* was a reply to Israel Mauduit's *Considerations on the present German War*.)

7. *An Answer to Lord Bolingbroke's Letters on the Study of History,* 1762, is often ascribed to HW. It was left in MS by his uncle, Horatio Walpole, 1st Baron Walpole; and published in 1762 by Lord Walpole's son, Horatio (1723–1809).

8. *Anecdotes of Polite Literature,* 5 vols., 1764. This anonymous compilation is attributed to HW in the old edition of Halkett and Laing's *Dictionary* and in Stonehill and Block's *Anonyma and Pseudonyma,* and therefore often catalogued as HW's. But see his letter to Cole, 7 February 1764, where he clearly says he does not know the author.

9. The Prologue to Jephson's *Count of Narbonne,* 1781, is attributed to HW in a contemporary newspaper (see Cole to HW, 11 February 1782), and by an unidentified collector who gathered up a number of HW's occasional verses. It was written by Jephson himself, who dedicated his play to HW. HW wrote to Cole, 14 February 1782, that the Prologue was not his but Jephson's.

10. A song, 'As the Mole's silent Stream,' printed in the *Morning Herald,* 20 November 1788, was marked 'By Mr. H. Walpole.' But in the Waller Collection there was a copy clipped from the newspaper and marked by HW 'Not by me.' In his miscellaneous *Book of Materials* now at the Folger Library, HW suggested that the song might be by his cousin Horatio (1752–1822).

11. A song, 'Rise, Cynthia, rise,' with music by Hook and words by 'Walpole, Earl of Orford,' was printed in William McCulloch's *Selected Music,* Philadelphia 1807, doubtless a reprint from an English collection. The song was written by HW's nephew, George, 3d Earl of Orford, and was included in his *Hasty Productions* 1791. (See the next entry.)

12. *Hasty Productions,* 1791. This volume of verses is included by Lowndes under HW's works. The author was HW's nephew, George, the third Earl.

13. 'A translation of verses found hanging upon a tablet in the Temple of Venus, in Lord Jersey's Wood, at Middleton Stoney. From the Latin of Horace Walpole, Esq.' I have seen only a clipping of these nineteen conventional lines, beginning 'Whoe'er thou art, whom chance ordains to rove,' but from the format it is possible to assume that they appeared in the *Morning Herald's* poetry column between 1780 and 1785. HW stopped briefly at Lord Jersey's in 1753 (see his letter to John Chute, 4 August 1753) and perhaps at other times. But 1780 seems an unlikely date for HW to be composing Latin verses. I think the Latin original is more likely to have been composed by HW's cousin, Horatio Walpole (1752–1822), who became 2d Earl of the 3d creation in 1809; he was at Eton 1764–70 and then at Trinity College, Cambridge (M.A. 1773).

14. *A full and particular account of a bloody duel . . . between C*[hetwynd] *and H*[orace] *W*[alpole], folio, single leaf, [1743]. This deals with the quarrel in which HW's uncle, Lord Walpole of Wolterton, was engaged. See HW to Horace Mann, 14 March 1743.

15. *Letter from an elector of the Borough of Great Yarmouth to Horatio*

APOCRYPHA

Walpole, 1730. This is catalogued under HW in the British Museum's Catalogue, but it was addressed to Lord Walpole of Wolterton. So was Thomas Secker's *Letter to Walpole,* written in 1751 but not published until 1769.

16. A number of other pieces creep into Walpolian lists because of their association with HW's uncle, Lord Walpole. *Considerations on the present state of affairs in Europe,* 1730, is probably by Lord Walpole; so are *The Case of the Hessian forces,* 1731, *The Convention vindicated,* 1739, and *The Grand question debated,* 1739. *The Case of the Hanover forces,* 1743, is probably by Chesterfield with some help from E. Waller; HW had two copies of it, but they contain no ascription of authorship; Lord Walpole wrote a reply called *The Interest of Great Britain steadily pursued.*

17. *The Impenetrable Secret.* See the *SH Bibliography,* pp. 145–148; I can now add slightly to the evidence accumulated there against the piece. Mr. H. Glenn Brown of the University of Pennsylvania Library has found Franklin's advertisement of it in the *Pennsylvania Gazette,* 11 May 1749, so that Hildeburn's accuracy is vindicated. Furthermore, George Bickham the engraver advertised the cards in January 1754, reduced from 10/6 to 2/6; and in June 1754 the third edition, with improvements, is offered for one shilling (*Daily Advertiser*). I think it is inconceivable that HW could have reprinted at SH a game that had been readily available to the public for more than ten years.

18. *The Opposition,* 1755. This pamphlet of twenty-eight pages is mentioned by Lowndes under HW, but unless the title was confused with HW's pamphlet of 1763 (described above), I do not know the reason for the attribution. HW had two copies, in one of which he wrote: 'Supposed to be by W. Gerard Hamilton.' It was published only a few weeks after Hamilton's celebrated speech of 13 November 1755.

19. In the eleventh volume of the *Political Register,* 1772, there is a letter to Lord Dartmouth on the Mississippi colonization scheme, dated 24 August 1772, and signed 'H. Walpole.' The style is not distinguished, and some statements sound quite unlike HW, so that the letter has been rejected by Mrs. Toynbee, Mr. Lewis, and other editors. If it is by HW, it is one of his poorer compositions. HW's cousin, Thomas Walpole (1727–1803), was a leader in the Ohio scheme of the same year, but internal evidence seems to rule him out as the writer, even if a misprint in the signature could be assumed. Possibly the letter was written by HW's twenty-year-old cousin Horatio (1752–1822), though this seems an unlikely guess.

UNPRINTED MANUSCRIPTS

The following list is far from complete, for it ignores many scattered scraps in various collections, such as the Berry Papers in the British Museum and in the Morgan Library, and it makes no reference to letters whether or not they include occasional poems. There are also extended notes in books, e.g., in Lysons's *Environs of London* and in Granger's *Biographical History* (described above). HW's copy of Sir John Hawkins's *History of Music,* with the fifth volume extensively annotated, is now at Farmington; according to Sir John's daughter Laetitia, it was HW who suggested to her father that he compile his *History.* The *Paris Journals* and the *Book of Visitors* have been published from MSS at Harvard, but many unpublished fragments and notes are at Harvard. Of three important MSS at the Folger Library (HW's *Books of Materials* containing a rich variety of biographical anecdotes, poetical fragments, and notes on the streets of London), only the notes on artists and a few miscellaneous extracts have been published. I specify below only the more important items in the Bentley Collection acquired by WSL in 1937: this great hoard of unpublished Walpolian MSS came mostly from Miss Berry, who seems to have sold them all to Richard Bentley the publisher when he was publishing HW's letters; and Mrs. Richard Bentley, widow of Bentley's descendant, sold them to WSL.

But the list represents fairly the unpublished independent works, and it will give some indication of the extent, the variety, and the titles of still-unpublished writings by HW. By comparing this list with the entries for works published since 1798, any reader can estimate what proportion of HW's miscellaneous writing is still waiting for publication.

In the *Waldegrave MS* (described briefly in the Introduction above) are numerous miscellaneous verses, many of them written in Italy and France, 1736–41, including 'Verses to John Dodd,' 1738; 'Verses to Zelinda from Florence' [*ca.* 1740]; and an imitation of Virgil: 'Sunday, or the Presence Chamber, a Town Eclogue.' Later pieces transcribed in the *Waldegrave MS* include an imitation of Horace: 'The Praises of a Poet's Life,' written in London in 1742; 'A Fairy Tale,' 1743; 'Little Peggy, a Prophetic Eclogue,' November 1743; more miscellaneous verses; a memoir of Ashton written about 1750; and notes about Dr. Conyers Middleton, Richard Bentley, and many others. The memoir of Ashton is prepared for publication in the fourteenth volume of the Yale edition of HW's *Correspondence.*

BIBLIOGRAPHY OF HORACE WALPOLE

Patapan, 1743. 'Short Notes': 'Summer [1743] I wrote *Patapan, or the Little White Dog,* a tale, imitated from Fontaine; it was never printed.' In the *Waldegrave MS* it is marked 'Wrote at Houghton 1743.'

Parody of Corneille's *Cinna,* 1744. 'Short Notes': In the summer of 1744 I wrote a parody of a scene in Corneille's *Cinna;* the interlocutors, Mr. Pelham, Mr. Arundel, and Mr. Selwyn.' In the *Waldegrave MS* it is marked 'Wrote in the summer of 1743.'

Imitation of Lucan, 1746. 'Short Notes': 'About the same time [end of 1746], I paraphrased some lines of the first book of Lucan; but they have not been printed.' HW's MS is now WSL, purchased in the Bentley Collection in 1937. His transcript in the *Waldegrave MS* is marked 'Windsor Octr. 1746. Addressed to Mr. Pitt.' This and the next poem were in HW's early MS list (now Morgan Library) of pieces to be included in his *Works,* but Miss Berry overlooked or rejected them.

Verses on the fireworks for the peace, 1749. 'Short Notes': '[In 1749] I wrote a copy of verses on the fireworks for the Peace; they were not printed.' HW's MS is now WSL, purchased in the Bentley Collection in 1937. His transcript is in the *Waldegrave MS*. Although in an early plan (*ca.* 1770) for his quarto *Works* (MS now in the Morgan Library), HW included this poem as well as the Imitation of Lucan, in a later list either by accident or design he omitted them.

Account of Mr. Chute and Miss Nicoll, 1751. 'Short Notes': 'About the same time [1751] happened a great family quarrel. My friend Mr. Chute had engaged Miss Nicoll, a most rich heiress, to run away from her guardians, who had used her very ill; and he proposed to marry her to my nephew, Lord Orford, who refused her, though she had above £150,000. . . . [I] wrote a particular account of the whole transaction.' See *Correspondence of Gray,* ed. Toynbee-Whibley, 1935, p. 356. The lady was Margaret Nicoll (or Nichol). HW's MS is now at Farmington, and a copy in an unidentified hand is at 'The Vyne' near Basingstoke. This MS is prepared for publication in the fourteenth volume of the Yale edition of HW's *Correspondence*.

'The Judgment of Solomon,' 1753. 'Short Notes': 'In November [1753] I wrote a burlesque poem, called the *Judgment of Solomon.*' HW's MS was in the Waller Collection; his transcript is in the *Waldegrave MS,* marked 'Nov. 1753.'

Account of his Conduct, in a letter to George, Earl of Orford, 1755. 'Short Notes': 'In March 1755 I was very ill used by my nephew Lord Orford, upon a contested election in the House of Commons, on which I wrote him a long letter, with an account of my own conduct in politics.' The letter seems not to have been preserved, although it may yet appear.

The Case of the Entail, 1756. 'Short Notes': 'In April 1756 my uncle Horace Walpole having drawn in my nephew Lord Orford to alter the settlement of his estate, I entered into a new dispute with my uncle on behalf of my nephews . . . and my sister . . .; and I wrote an account of that whole affair.' HW's account in MS is at Farmington.

Epitaph for Lady Townshend's youngest son, 1759. 'Short Notes': 'September 21st [1759]. I gave my Lady Townshend an epitaph and design for a

UNPRINTED MANUSCRIPTS

tomb for her youngest son, killed at Ticonderoga; neither were used.' The MS of HW's brief epitaph, together with Bentley's sketch (from HW's design) for the tomb, and the letter to Lady Townshend were purchased from Maggs Bros. by WSL in August 1946.

'Destruction of the French Navy,' 1760. 'Short Notes': 'April [1760]. In this month wrote a poem on the Destruction of the French Navy, as an exercise for Lord Beauchamp at Christchurch, Oxford.' The MS is still untraced.

'To Britannia,' 1764. HW included this long verse satire in his MS list (now Morgan Library) of the pieces to be included in his *Works*. A copy not in his hand but with one note apparently by him is now at Farmington, purchased by WSL in 1937 in the Bentley Collection.

'Thoughts on keeping holy the Sabbath, by J. Cardan.' Kirgate gave Miss Berry a copy of this in his hand (now in the Berry Papers in the British Museum) to be included in the *Works* of 1798, but she rejected it; HW listed it as one of the pieces to be included (MS now in the Morgan Library: see *SH Bibliography*, p. 89).

Among the Berry Papers in the Morgan Library, besides smaller scraps, there are the following pieces: 'Character of George, Lord Lyttelton'; 'Loose Thoughts,' three pages on the philosophy of kingship; 'Life of the King of Naples,' 1779; and 'George III and his Ministers,' a summary written in June 1785.

At Farmington, besides many smaller scraps, there are the following pieces, largely from the Bentley Collection: Notes on the sessions of Parliament, 1744–45; 'Memoirs from the Declaration of the War with Spain,' *ca.* 1746; Notes of an interview with the Prince of Wales, 2 March 1748; Portrait of Lord Mansfield; 'Address on the King's Speech, 13 November 1761,' reworked into his *Memoirs of George III*; 'History of Mme. Du Barry,' 1769; 'Abstract of the Kings and Queens of England,' *ca.* 1770 (five pages but imperfect); Character of Wedderburn, 1771; Reply to James Barry's attack about the Dutch painters, *ca.* 1775; 'The Junto,' verses dated 1777 (in the MS of 'Short Notes' this is put under 1778 but then bracketed as if out of place: 'In the winter wrote the Junto, a poem'); Character of the 5th Duke of Devonshire, *ca.* 1780; 'The Spirit of the Present Reign,' *ca.* 1780; 'Sketch of a History written in a method entirely new, by John Short, Gent.,' *ca.* 1783 (a fragmentary first draft of this satire was printed by Dr. Doran in the *Last Journals*, for July 1782); *Memoirs of the Reign of George III*, 1783–1791 (now prepared for publication); 'Instructions to my Successors at SH,' 1771–1785, and 'Directions for publishing,' 1794–1796; Character of King George III, *ca.* 1788; and numerous receipts signed by HW. Also at Farmington is the MS of 'Short Notes,' differing very considerably from the text published by Richard Bentley in the Mann *Letters*, 1843; this MS is now prepared for publication in the thirteenth volume of the Yale edition of HW's *Correspondence*.

'On the Duchess of Kingston's going to Rome,' *ca.* 1774. This twelve-line poem is known only from a copy, at Farmington, taken from Kirgate's MSS.

Letter to the *Gazetteer* on bee-keeping in Spain. The material for this letter came from the Earl of Sandwich's diary, which HW examined in the winter of 1761–62 (see HW to the Earl of Egremont, 20 April 1762). The letter is signed 'Apicius,' and endorsed in pencil 'No. 9 1761.' 'To the Printer of the *London Chronicle*' was HW's first heading; then the *Gazetteer* was substituted. It is not impossible that the letter was published, but no file of the *Gazetteer* is readily available. WSL bought the MS at Sotheby's, 15 November 1932 (Property of Mrs. Erskine, grandniece of Grosvenor Charles Bedford).

'Lines on the New Front of Wentworth Castle.' See HW's 'Journals of Visits to Country Seats' in the sixteenth volume of the Walpole Society, 1927–28, p. 28: '[August 1760. Lord Strafford] has begun a much more beautiful side front'; also p. 65: '[September 1768, at Lord Strafford's] I had been there before, but had not seen the new front, entirely designed by the present Earl himself. Nothing ever came up to the beauty of it. The grace, proportion, lightness, and magnificence of it are exquisite.' It is likely that HW composed his verses in September 1768 or soon afterwards. He included 'Lines on the new front of Wentworth Castle' in his list (written *ca.* 1780) of verses to be printed in his quarto *Works,* and again in a list drawn up in 1790 or later (MSS in the Morgan Library). Perhaps Miss Berry rejected the poem or perhaps HW later decided not to preserve it. I do not think it was ever published, and although the MS may well exist, I have not traced it.

Henry Seymour Conway wrote to HW, 6 August 1740 (printed in Lord Albemarle's *Memoirs of Rockingham,* 1852, i.374): 'Your ballad is extremely pretty, and I think you have done it great injury to put it up in that halfpenny form, with such a title, and a frontispiece that I could have done myself.' HW was in Italy at this time. Since we have no knowledge of anything published by HW in this period, it is possible that the letter refers to a MS sent by HW to Conway. If the text was of HW's composition, this would represent an unidentified poem by HW.

HW wrote to Lord Hertford, 12 February 1765: 'If it was not too long to transcribe, I would send you an entertaining petition of the Perriwig makers to the King, in which they complain that men will wear their own hair. Should one almost wonder if carpenters were to remonstrate, that since the peace their trade decays, and that there is no demand for wooden legs?' Croker's note on this passage, in 1825, calls attention to the 'Historical Chronicle' for 11 February in the *Gentleman's Magazine* for February 1765, in which it is reported that a petition of the master peruke-makers was presented to the King, setting forth the distresses 'occasioned by the present mode of men in all stations wearing their own hair, [etc.]' The 'Historical Chronicle' continues: 'In ridicule of the barbers, a petition from the company of *body Carpenters,* as they are called, was ludicrously framed, imploring his majesty to wear a wooden leg himself, and to enjoin all his servants to appear . . . with the same badge of honor, &c.' Croker says: 'It may be presumed that this *jeu d'esprit* was from the pen of Mr. Walpole.' Such an attribution seems not unreasonable; but unless the comic petition was printed in a newspaper of the day, it must be counted as an unprinted and (at present) a lost MS.

INDEX

Abbreviations 13, 14.
'Abstract of the Kings and Queens of England' 177.
Account of his Conduct, in a letter to George, Earl of Orford 176.
Account of Mr. Chute and Miss Nicoll 176.
Account of my Conduct 82.
Account of the Giants 67–69.
Additional papers relative to Chatterton 82.
'Address on the King's Speech' 177.
Address to the Public on the Late Dismission of a General Officer 50.
Advertisement for a History of Good Breeding 155.
Advertisement of the She-Witch from Lapland 153.
Advertisements by HW. *See* Prefaces.
'Advice, The' 84.
Aedes Walpolianae 10, 26–32.
Akenside, Mark, editor 155.
Almon, John (1737–1805), publisher 50; *Biographical, Literary, and Political Anecdotes* 47, 159, 162; *Collection of Scarce and Interesting Tracts* 50; *Debates of the House of Commons* 155; *History of the late Minority* 47; *Review of Lord Bute's Administration* 47; *Review of Mr. Pitt's Administration* 47.
Andrews, Miles Peter 169.
Anecdotes of Painting 9, 45, 48.
Anecdotes of Polite Literature 172.
Anecdotes told me by Lady Denbigh 101.
Annesley, Francis (d. 1812) 147.
Answer from Lien Chi in Pekin to Xo Ho 41.

Answer to Lord Bolingbroke's Letters on the Study of History 172.
'Apicius' *pseud.* of HW 178.
'As the Mole's silent Stream' 172.
Ashton, Thomas (1716–75) 156, 175; HW's letters to 93.
Asylum for Fugitive Pieces 164.
Authentick Copy of the last Will and Testament [of Robert Earl of Orford] 110.

Baker, Rev. Thomas (1656–1740) 81, 82.
Ballad, HW's, referred to 178.
Banks, John, editor 154.
Bannerman, Alexander 170.
Barebone, Issachar, *pseud. See* Ralph, James.
Barker, G. F. R., editor 95.
Barnardiston, Hester 52.
Barry, James, painter, HW's reply to 177.
Bartholomew, Augustus Theodore (1882–1933) 48.
Bath, Earl of. *See* Pulteney, William.
Bathoe, William (d. 1768), publisher 41, 47, 48, 49, 54, 55, 120–124.
Beauclerk, Lady Diana (Spencer) (1734–1808) 84.
Beauties, The 22–24, 156.
Becket, Thomas, publisher 45, 132, 142.
Bedford, Grosvenor 31.
Bedford, John Russell (1766–1839), 6th Duke of 87.
Bee-keeping, HW's letter on 177.
Bell and Bradfute, publishers 89.
Bensley, Thomas (d. 1833), printer 145.
Bentley, Richard (1708–82) 93, 175, 177; *Designs for Six Poems by Gray: see*

[179]

INDEX

Gray, Thomas; *Designs for Walpole's Fugitive Pieces* 43, 101; *Reflections on Cruelty* 47, 128–130.
Bentley, Richard (1794–1871), publisher 66, 91, 93, 96, 97, 157, 175.
Bentley, Mrs. Richard, Collection of MSS 93, 152, 157, 163, 175, 176, 177.
Berkeley, Lady Elizabeth. *See* Craven, Elizabeth Berkeley, Lady.
Berry, Mary (1763–1852) 56, 72, 75, 141, 166, 175–178; Letters of HW to 91, 93.
Berry, Robert 75.
Bibliography of the Strawberry Hill Press 7, 8, 9; Corrections to 11–13.
Bickham, George, engraver 173.
Birch, George 52, 57, 62.
Birrell, A., engraver 61, 63.
Blackwood, William (1776–1836), publisher 89.
Blizard, Sir William, 'Stanzas on viewing Strawberry Hill' 169.
Bodoni, Giambattista (1740–1813), printer 56–62.
Bone, Henry, *Catalogue of Miniature Portraits at Woburn Abbey* 87.
Bonfoy, Nicholas (d. 1775) 49.
Book of Visitors 175.
Books of Materials 166, 175.
Boswell, James 134.
Brown, H. Glenn 173.
Buck (Buc), Sir George (d. 1623), *History of Richard III* 69.
Buckingham, Duke of. *See* Villiers, George (1628–87).
Burrell, Lady, *Lines sent to Mr. Walpole* 170.
Bute, John Stuart (1713–92), 3d E. of 45.
Butler, John (1717–1802), Bishop of Hereford, *Serious Considerations on the Measures of the Present Administration* 49.

Cadell, Thomas (1742–1802), publisher 71, 132.
Cambridge University, *Gratulatio* 105–107.
Campbell, Lady Mary (1727–1811), *m.* Edward Coke: HW's verses to 52, 54; HW's Mock sermon to 166.

'Card to Lady Blandford' 84.
Caroline (1683–1737), Queen of England, Pictures of 122, 123.
Carter, John, *Specimens of Ancient Sculpture and Painting* 169.
Case of the Entail 176.
Case of the Hanover Forces 173.
Case of the Hessian Forces 173.
Castle of Otranto 8, 9, 48, 52–67.
Catalogue of Pictures and Drawings in the Holbein Chamber 45.
Catalogue of Pictures of Charles I 120–122.
Catalogue of the Pictures belonging to James II 122, 123.
Catalogue of the Pictures belonging to the Duke of Buckingham 122, 124.
Catalogue of the Royal and Noble Authors of England 9, 42, 48, 81.
Catherine (1485–1536) of Aragon, Q. of Henry VIII 164.
Chamber(s), Anna. *See* Temple.
Chanson on Lady Caroline Petersham and Col. Conway 166.
'Character of George, Lord Lyttelton' 177.
Character of King George III 177.
Character of the 5th Duke of Devonshire 177.
Character of Wedderburn 177.
Charles I, King of England, Catalogue of Pictures of 120–122.
Chesterfield, Philip Dormer Stanhope (1694–1773), 4th E. of: *Case of the Hanover Forces* 173; contributes to the *World* 157; letters of 9; HW's Notes on his *Works* 98, 99; Parody of 83.
Chronicle of the Kings of England 19.
Chute, John (1701–76) 176.
Clarke, Anne Melicent, *m.* (1802) E. H. Delmé 61, 63, 64.
Classic Memoirs 95.
Clive, Catherine (1711–85) 164; HW's Epilogue spoken by 163.
Coke, Lady Mary. *See* Campbell, Lady Mary.
Colburn, Henry, publisher 89, 91, 149, 151.
Cole, Rev. William (1714–82) 52, 130, 143; HW's letters to 89, 90.

[180]

INDEX

Commonplace Book of Horace Walpole's 98.
Congratulatory Letter to Selim 34.
Considerations on the present dangerous Crisis (Ruffhead) 45.
Considerations on the present German War 171.
Considerations on the present state of affairs in Europe 173.
'Constant Correspondent, A' *pseud.* of HW 162.
Continuation of Baker's Chronicle 83.
Convention vindicated, The 173.
Conway, Francis Seymour (1719–94), E. of Hertford 91.
Conway, Henry Seymour (1719–95), General 50, 178; HW's verses to 159.
Cooper, Mary, publisher 24, 25, 32, 34, 43, 48, 111.
Cornbury, Henry Hyde, Lord. See Hyde, Henry.
Correspondence of HW 9, 11, 84, 85; Collected editions of 91, 92.
Corticchiato, Dominique 67.
Counter-Address to the Public 47, 50–52.
'Countess Temple appointed Poet Laureate' 84.
Craven, Elizabeth Berkeley (1750–1828), Baroness 61; *Modern Anecdote* 169; translation of the *Sleep-Walker* 141.
Crewe, Robert Offley Ashburton Crewe-Milnes (1858–1945), E. of 12.
Criticism on Johnson 83.
Croker, John Wilson (1780–1857), editor 91, 178.
Cumming, John, publisher 89.
Cunningham, Peter (1816–69), editor 93.

D., C., correspondent of *European Magazine* 87.
Davies, Thomas (1712?–85), publisher 131–134, 137, 138, 142.
'Dear Witches,' in *Old England* 153.
Dedications by HW. See Prefaces.
Defense of Mr. Rousseau. See Greene, Edward Burnaby.
'Delenda est Oxonia' 166.
Description of the Villa 49, 75.
Description of the Works of Hollar 125.

Descriptive Catalogue of the Portraits . . . at Woburn Abbey 87.
Designs by Mr. R. Bentley for Six Poems by Mr. T. Gray. See Gray, Thomas.
Desmond, Countess of. See Fitzgerald, Catherine.
'Destruction of the French Navy' 177.
Detached Pieces printed at SH 12, 13.
Detached Thoughts 83.
'Detection of a late Forgery' [*Testament Politique*] 81.
Devonshire, William (1748–1811), 5th Duke of, his Character by HW 177.
Dialogue between two great Ladies 43–45, 48.
Dickenson, Mrs. Mary (Hamilton) (1756–1816) 62.
'Directions for publishing' 177.
'Dissertation on the Liberty of the Press' in *Old England* 171.
Dobson, Austin 149.
Dodsley, James (1724–97), publisher 56, 71, 139, 140, 142.
Dodsley, Robert (1703–64), publisher 9, 24, 25, 30, 48, 110–112, 114–117, 155, 157; his *Collection of Poems* 24, 26, 156.
Doran, John (1807–78), editor 75.
Dover, George James Welbore Agar-Ellis (1797–1833), first Baron, editor 91.
Duchess of Portland's Museum 101.
Du Deffand, Marie de Vichy-Champrond (1696–1780), Letters of 93.
Dyce Collection 28.

Eckardt (Eccardt), John Giles (*d.* 1779) 22, 115.
Edward VI, King of England, Letters 136.
Edwards, James (1757–1816), bookseller 56, 76, 77.
Eidous, Marc Antoine 55.
Elegy wrote in a Country Church Yard 110–113.
English Connoisseur 31.
'Entail, The' 43.
Epigram on Admiral Vernon 43.
Epigrams 84.
Epilogue to *Braganza*, HW's 136.
Epilogue to Mrs. Griffith's *The Times*, HW's 84, 141–143.

[181]

INDEX

Epilogue to *Tamerlane,* HW's 24–26, 52, 156.
Epilogues. *See also* Prologues and Epilogues.
Epistle for the Day 22.
'Epistle from Florence to Thomas Ashton' 156.
Epitaph for Lady Townshend's youngest Son 176, 177.
'Epitaph on Lady Ossory's Bullfinches' 84.
Epitaph on Mrs. Clive's Monument 164.
Epitaph on the Cenotaph of Lady Walpole 43.
'Epitaphium vivi auctoris' 84.
Essay on Modern Gardening 75.
Essay on the Liberty of the Press 171.
Essex, George Capel (1757–1839), 5th E. of 149.
Essex, James (1722–84), architect 164.
Etchings by Lady Louisa Augusta Greville 13.
Evans, Thomas (d. 1784), publisher 137–138.
Evelyn, Elizabeth 22.
Evening Lessons, The, being the First and Second Chapters of the Book of Entertainments 22.
Evening Lessons for the Day 21.

Fairfax, Brian (1633–1711) 124.
'Fairy Tale, A' 175.
Farren, Eliza (1759?–1829), later Countess of Derby 141.
Felton, Samuel, *Imperfect Hints toward a new Edition of Shakespeare* 169.
Ferrers, Laurence Shirley (1720–60), 4th Earl 43.
Fitz-Adam, Adam, *pseud. See* Moore, Edward.
Fitzgerald, Catherine (d. 1604), Countess of Desmond 43.
Forlorn Printer . . . Thomas Kirgate, The 101.
Foundling Hospital for Wit, Pieces reprinted in the 21, 22, 26, 36, 39.
Four Letters published in Old England 154.
Fox, Lady Caroline (1723–74) 22, 157.

Fox, Henry (1705–74), later Lord Holland 22, 157.
Fox, Henry Richard Vassall (1773–1840), 3d Baron Holland, editor 95.
Francklin, Richard (d. 1765), printer 158.
Fraser, Sir William Augustus (1826–98), editor 98, 100.
Frederick Louis, Prince of Wales (1707–51), Verses on his marriage 105–107.
Fugitive Pieces 41, 42, 43.
Fugitive Verses, Horace Walpole's, ed. by W. S. Lewis 9, 98, and *passim.*
Full and particular Account of a bloody Duel between [Chetwynd and Horace Walpole] 172.
'Funeral of the Lioness' 83.

'Garland, The' 165.
Gatty, Hugh 167.
Genuine Copy of a Letter found near Strawberry Hill 170.
'George III and his Ministers' 177.
George III, King of England, his Character by HW 177.
Gibbon, Edward 72.
Gilpin, William, *Essay on Prints* 169.
Goldsmith, Oliver 41.
Gough, Richard (1735–1809) 73, 125; *Sepulchral Monuments* 143–145.
Graham, Josiah, publisher 41, 48.
Grammont (Gramont), Comte de, *Mémoires* 136.
Grand Question Debated, The 173.
Granger, James (1723–76), *Biographical History of England* 130–136, 169, 175; *Letters* 130.
Grangerizing 134, 135.
Gratulatio Academiae Cantabrigiensis 105–107.
Gray, Thomas 9, 30, 156; *Designs by Mr. R. Bentley for Six Poems by* 10, 113–120; *Elegy* 9, 110–113; HW's letters to 93; 'Memoir' by HW 165; *Ode on a Distant Prospect of Eton College* 110; *Poems,* ed. Mason 138–141; 'Seeds of Poetry and Rhime' attributed to 166.
Greathead (Greatheed), Bertie (1759–1826) 62.

[182]

INDEX

Greene, Edward Burnaby, *Defense of Mr. Rousseau*, dedicated to HW 161.
Griffith, Mrs. Elizabeth (1720?-93), *The Times* 141-143.
Griffiths, Ralph (1720-1803), editor 116.
Guidickens, Frederick William (d. 1779), Answer to Mr. Walpole's Late Work [*Historic Doubts*] 73.
Gulliver's Travels, Sequel to 165.
Guthrie, William, editor 154; *Address to the Public* 50; *Reply to the Counter-Address* 50.

Hamilton, Anthony (ca. 1645-1720). See Grammont, Comte de.
Hamilton, William Gerard (1729-96) 173.
Hardwicke, Earl of. See Yorke.
Hawkesworth, John 155.
Hawkins, Sir John, *History of Music* 175.
Hawthorne, J., his copy of Hentzner's *Journey* 147.
Hawtrey, Edward Craven (1789-1862) 72.
Hayter, Thomas 171.
Heath, James (1757-1834), engraver 79.
Heathcote, Ralph, *Letter to Walpole* 162.
Hentzner, Paul, *Journey* 125, 147, 148.
Herbert of Cherbury, Edward, Lord, *Life* 130.
Hertford, Francis Seymour Conway (1719-94), created (1750) Earl of, HW's letters to 91.
Hieroglyphic Tales 75, 165.
Historic Doubts on Richard III 69-74.
'History of Mme. Du Barry' 177.
Hobson, G. D. 63.
Hoey, James, bookseller in Dublin 54.
Holbein Chamber, Catalogue of Pictures and Drawings in 45.
Holland. See Fox.
Hollar, Wenceslaus (1607-77), engraver 125.
Howard, H., *Choice Spirits Museum* 159.
Hoyland, Francis, *Poems* 130.
Hughs, John (d. 1771), printer 30.
Hume, David 72, 83, 160.
Hyde, Henry (1710-53), Viscount Cornbury, *The Mistakes* 125-127, 147.

Imitation of Lucan, by HW 176.
Impenetrable Secret 173.

Inscription for the Neglected Column at Florence 42.
Inscription on a Picture of the late Pope 43.
'Instructions to my Successors at SH' 177.
Interest of Great Britain steadily pursued 173.
Introductions by HW. See Prefaces.
Isabelle et Théodore 65.
Ives, John, *Select Papers* 169.

James II, King of England, Catalogue of Pictures of 122, 123.
Jeffery, Edward, publisher 65, 80, 149.
Jephson, Robert (1736-1803), *Braganza* 136-138; *Count of Narbonne* 56, 169, 172.
Jerningham, Edward (1727-1812) 165; *The Swedish Curate* 169.
Johnson, Samuel 117, 134, 157.
Journal of the Printing Office 98.
Journal of the Reign of George III 95-97.
'Journals of Visits to Country Seats' 166.
Journey to Houghton. See Whaley, John.
'Judgment of Solomon' 176.
Junot, Maréchal Andache (1771-1813), Duc d'Abrantes 61.
Junto, The 177.

Kearsley, George, publisher 49.
Ketton-Cremer, R. W. 149.
Kirgate, Thomas, printer 12, 45, 47, 62, 79, 87, 101, 115, 120, 128, 164.
Knapton, John and Paul, publishers 108.
Knight, Charles (1791-1873), publisher 91.
Knight, E. Cornelia, *Marcus Flaminius* 169.

Langley, William, Mayor of Lynn 162.
Lawrence, Sir Thomas (1769-1830), painter 79.
Lea and Blanchard, publishers 95.
Le Marchant, Sir Denis (1795-1874), editor 95.
Lennox, Lady Georgiana Caroline. See Fox, Lady Caroline.
Lesson for the Day (by Michael Ben Haddi) 22.
Lessons for Evening Service 22.
Lessons for the Day 19-22.

INDEX

Letter from Madame de Sévigné, HW's 101.
Letter from the King of Prussia to Rousseau 8, 160–162.
Letter from Xo Ho 39–42, 48.
Letter to Horace Walpole 172, 173.
Letter to the Editor of . . . Chatterton 75.
Letter to the *Gazetteer* on Bee-keeping in Spain 177.
Letter to the Mayor of Lynn 162.
Letter to the Tories 32.
Letter to the Whigs 32–34, 49.
Letters 84, 85.
Letters of Edward VI 136.
Letters of HW, Collected editions of 91, 92.
Letters to and from Ministers 82.
Letters to and from Richard West 84.
Letters to Cole 89, 90.
Letters to George Montagu 87–89.
Letters to the Earl of Hertford 91.
Lewis, Lady Maria Theresa (1803–65), editor 93, 166.
Lewis, Wilmarth S., editor 93, 98, 101.
Liberty of the Press, Essays on, attributed to HW 171.
Liddell, Anne (1738–1804), Lady Ossory, HW's letters to 91.
Lien Chi 41.
Life of Edward, Lord Herbert of Cherbury 9, 130.
Life of Rev. Thomas Baker 81, 82.
'Life of the King of Naples' 177.
Lines on the Duchess of Queensbury 163.
'Lines on the New Front of Wentworth Castle' 178.
'Lines to Lady Anne Fitzpatrick' 84.
'Little Peggy, a Prophetic Eclogue' 175.
'Loose Thoughts' 177.
Louis XVI, King of France 72.
Lowndes (Lownds), Thomas (1719–84), publisher 52, 54.
Lysons, Daniel (1762–1834), *Environs of London* 169, 175.
Lyttelton, George (1709–73), later Lord Lyttelton 32; his Character by HW 177.

Maclure, Colonel Alan F. 98.
Magazines. *See* Periodicals.
Malcolm, James Peller (1767–1815), editor 130.
Mann, Sir Horace, Letters of HW to 91.
Mansfield, William Murray (1705–93), Earl of, his Portrait by HW 177.
Manuscripts by HW, Unpublished 11, 175.
Marshall, William 52.
Martin, John, editor 87, 89.
Mason, William (1725–97), editor of Gray's *Poems* 138–141; *Heroic Epistle* 49, 152; *Heroic Postscript* 152; HW's letters to 91; *Satirical Poems with Notes by HW* 152.
Masters, Robert (1713–98), *Some Remarks on Historic Doubts* 73.
Mauduit, Israel 171.
Mead, Richard (1673–1754) 48, 134.
Medalist, The 171.
Medland, Thomas (*d.* 1833), engraver 64.
Meil, J. W., engraver 63.
Memoir of Gray, by HW 165.
Memoires of the Reign of George II 84, 85, 93, 95.
'Memoirs from the Declaration of the War with Spain' 177.
Memoirs of Horace Walpole and his Contemporaries 149, 151.
Memoirs of the Reign of George III 48, 49, 93, 95, 96, 160.
Memoirs of the Reign of George III, 1783–1791 177.
Memoirs of the Reigns of George II and George III 8, 93–97.
Memoranda Walpoliana 101.
Mendez, Jael 163.
Mendez, Moses, *Collection of the most esteemed Pieces of Poetry* 163.
Middleton, Dr. Conyers 175.
Middleton, N., publisher 41.
Milles, Jeremiah (1714–84), Dean of Exeter, 'Observations on the Wardrobe Account' 73.
Miscellaneous Antiquities 136.
'Miscellaneous Antiquities,' ed. by W. S. Lewis 43, 98, 101.
Miser, The 170.
Mississippi Colonization Scheme 173.
Mistakes, The 125–127.

[184]

INDEX

Mitford, John (1781–1859), editor 91, 165.
Mock Sermon to Lady Mary Coke 166.
Montagu, Lord Frederick (1774–1827) 89.
Montagu, George, Letters of HW to 87–89.
Moody, Elizabeth, 'On the Death of Horace Walpole' 170.
Moore, Edward, editor 157; *Trial of Selim the Persian* 34.
More, Hannah, *Florio* 169.
Mountstuart, Lord. See Stuart, John (1744–1814).
Müller (Miller), Johann Sebastian (1715?–90?), engraver 115.
Müntz, John Henry, painter 93.
Muralto, Onuphrio 52.
Murphy, Arthur, Prologue to *Braganza* 136.
Murray, John (1745–93), publisher 55, 94.
Murray, John (1778–1843), publisher 89.
Museum, The 155.
Mysterious Mother 74.

Narrative of the Quarrel between Hume and Rousseau 83.
Nature Will Prevail 81.
New Foundling Hospital for Wit, pieces reprinted in 42, 43, 159, 163, 164.
New Lesson for Pope 22.
Newspapers, Contributions by HW to:
 Advertisement of the She-Witch from Lapland (*Daily Advertiser*) 153.
 Epilogue spoken by Mrs. Clive (*Public Advertiser*) 163.
 Epitaph on Mrs. Clive's Monument (*London Evening Post*) 164.
 Letter from King of Prussia (*St. James's Chronicle*) 160.
 Letter on Bee-keeping in Spain (*Gazetteer*) 177.
 Letter to Mayor of Lynn (*St. James's Chronicle*) 162.
 Letters (*Public Advertiser*) 162.
 Political papers (*London Evening Post*) 159, 160.
 'The Three Vernons' (*St. James's Chronicle*) 164.
 Verses for the Monument of Queen Catherine (*Public Advertiser*) 164.
 Verses occasioned by a late Will (*London Evening Post*) 155.
 Verses to General Conway (*Public Advertiser*) 159.
Nichols, John (1745–1826), publisher 144, 145.
Nicoll (Nichol), Margaret 176.
Noble, Francis (d. 1792), publisher 67.
Noble, Rev. Mark (1754–1827), editor, *Biographical History of England* 134, 135.
Norfolk Tour 31.
North Briton 50.
Notes by Horace Walpole on Several Characters of Shakespeare 101.
Notes of an interview with the Prince of Wales 177.
Notes on Lord Chesterfield's Works 98, 99.
'Notes on the Exhibitions of the Society of Artists and the Free Society' 167.
Notes on the Poems of Alexander Pope 98, 100.
Notes on the sessions of Parliament 177.
Notes to the Portraits at Woburn Abbey 85–87.

'On Seeing Strawberry Hill' 170.
'On the Duchess of Kingston's going to Rome' 177.
Opposition, The 173.
Opposition to the late Minister Vindicated 45–50.
Orford, George, 3d Earl, *Hasty Productions* 172.
Orford, Horace Walpole, 4th Earl of. See under Walpole, and *passim* under titles of his works.
Original Speech of Sir William Stanhope 36, 37.
Osborn, Danvers 31.
Ossory, Lady. See Liddell, Anne.

'Parallel of Sir Robert Walpole and Mr. Pelham' 95.
Paris Journals 166, 167, 175.
'Parish Register of Twickenham' 83.
Park, Thomas (1759–1834), editor 42.
Parody of Corneille's *Cinna* 176.

INDEX

Parody of Lord Chesterfield's *Letters* 83.
Patapan 176.
Patch, Thomas, *Life of Fra Bartolommeo* 170.
Payne, Thomas (1719–99), publisher 144.
'Peach in Brandy, The' 165.
Percy, Thomas (1729–1811), Bishop of Dromore 55.
Periodicals, Contributions by HW to:
    Essay in Ralph's *Protester* 158.
    Essays in Dodsley's *Museum* 155.
    Essays in *Old England* 153, 154.
    Essays in the *Remembrancer* 156, 157.
    Essays in the *World* 157, 158.
    'The Garland' in *Quarterly Review* 165.
    Lines on Duchess of Queensbury in *Gentleman's Magazine* 163.
    Speech in Parliament in *London Magazine* 155.
    'Strawberry Hill, a Ballad' in *Gentleman's Magazine* 158.
    Verses to Edward Jerningham in *European Magazine* 165.
Phillips, Richard (1767–1840), publisher 145, 146.
Philo-Briton, his Letter to Lien Chi 41.
Pindar, Peter, *pseud. See* Wolcot, John.
Pinkerton, John, *Walpoliana* 145–147, 149; *Essay on Medals* 170.
Piozzi, Mrs. Hester Lynch (Thrale), marginal notes in *Letters to Montagu* 85.
Pitt, William (1708–78), later E. of Chatham 45.
Political Register 173.
Pont-de-Veyle, Comte de, translation of his *Somnambule* by Lady Craven 141.
Poole, Austin Lane, editor 117–119.
Pope, Alexander, HW's notes on his *Works* 98, 100.
Porter, Mary (d. 1765) 127, 147.
Portrait of Lord Mansfield 177.
Portrait of Mme. du Deffand 84.
Postscript to *Historic Doubts* 73, 78, 81.
Postscript to *Royal and Noble Authors* 42.
'Praises of a Poet's Life' 175.
Pratt, William, printer 48.
Prefaces by HW, Books with:
    Bentley's *Designs for Six Poems by Gray* 113–120.
    Bentley's *Reflections on Cruelty* 128–130.
    Catalogue of Pictures belonging to James the Second 122, 123.
    Catalogue of Pictures belonging to the Duke of Buckingham 122, 124.
    Catalogue of Pictures of Charles the First 120–122.
    Gray's *Elegy* 110–113.
    Gray's *Poems* with Designs by Bentley 113–120.
    Hentzner's *Journey* 125, 147.
    Hoyland's *Poems* 130.
    Lady Temple's *Poems* (Prefatory verses) 130.
    Letters of Edward the Sixth 136.
    Life of Lord Herbert of Cherbury 130.
    Lord Cornbury's *Mistakes* 125–127.
    Mémoires du Comte de Grammont 136.
    Miscellaneous Antiquities 136.
    Sleep-Walker (Prefatory verses) 141.
    Whitworth's *Account of Russia* 128.
Private Correspondence of HW 91.
Proby, Major R. G. 62.
Proclamation, A, a Poem 171.
Prologue and Epilogue to the *Mysterious Mother* 84.
Prologue to the *Count of Narbonne* attributed to HW 172.
Prologues and Epilogues by HW:
    Epilogue spoken by Mrs. Clive 163.
    Epilogue to *Braganza* 136.
    Epilogue to *Tamerlane* 24–26, 52, 156.
    Epilogue to *The Times* 84, 141.
    Prologue and Epilogue to the *Mysterious Mother* 84.
Protester, The 158.
Pulteney, William (1684–1764), cr. (1742) E. of Bath 19, 158, 159.
Pye, Mrs. J. Henrietta (Mrs. Robert Hampden Pye), *Poems* 163.

Queensbury, Catherine Douglas (d. 1777), Duchess of 163.

Ralph, James (1705?–62), editor 157, 158.
Rambler, The 157.
Ranby, John (1703–73), *Narrative of the last Illness of Lord Orford* 107–109.

INDEX

Redmond, Jean de (*ca.* 1709–78), Lieutenant General 69.
Reed, Isaac (1742–1807) 128.
Rees-Mogg, W. 81.
Reflections on Cruelty 128–130.
Remembrancer, The 156, 157.
Reminiscences 83, 145.
Reply to Dean Milles, HW's 73, 75.
Reply to Mr. Robert Masters, HW's 73.
'Retreat for the Gods, A' 170.
Reveley, Willey (*d.* 1799) 61.
Reynolds, Sir Joshua 169.
Richardson, Samuel (1689–1761), publisher 126.
Riddles by HW 84.
Ripley, Thomas, *Plans, Elevations and Sections . . . of Houghton* 31.
'Rise, Cynthia, rise,' a song 172.
Robinson, G. G. and J., publishers 76, 77.
Rodwell and Martin, publishers 89, 91.
Rousseau, Jean Jacques 83, 160.
Rowe, Nicholas, Epilogue by HW to his *Tamerlane*. See Epilogue.
Ruffhead, Owen (1723–69), writer 45.
Russell, John, 6th D. of Bedford. See Bedford.

Sackville, Lord George (1716–85) 43.
Scheme for a Tax on Message Cards 155.
Secker, Thomas, *Letter to Walpole* 173.
Second and Third Letter to the Whigs 34–36.
'Seeds of Poetry and Rhime' 166.
Seeley, Leonard Benton (1831–93), *Horace Walpole and his World* 149.
Select Observations 101.
Sequel to Gulliver's Travels 165.
Sermon on Painting 26.
Sharpe, John, publisher 145.
Sherburn, George 98.
She-Witch from Lapland, Pretended Advertisement of 153.
'Short Notes' 14, 177.
Sivrac, George 61.
'Sketch of a History by John Short, Gent.' 177.
Sleep-Walker, The 141.
Smith, Robert Vernon (1800–73), editor 91, 165.

Sonnet to Lady Mary Coke, HW's 54, 57.
Spectator, The, parody of by HW 165.
Speech in Parliament on the Hanoverian Troops 154, 155.
Speech of Richard White-Liver 38, 39.
Speech without Doors 36.
Spencer, John (*d.* 1746), HW's verses on his will 155.
'Spirit of the Present Reign' 177.
Stanhope, Sir William (1702–72) 36.
Stokes, Francis Griffin, editor 112.
Strafford, Earl of. See Wentworth.
'Strawberry Hill, a Ballad' 158, 159.
Strawberry Hill Accounts 98.
Strawberry Hill Bibliography. See *Bibliography of the SH Press*.
Stuart, John. See Bute, John Stuart (1713–92), 3d E. of.
Stuart, John (1744–1814), Viscount Mountstuart, purchases Granger's MSS 134.
Suard, Jean-Baptiste-Antoine (1733–1817), *Exposé succinct de la contestation entre M. Hume et M. Rousseau* 161.
Summers, Rev. Montague, editor 67.
'Sunday, or The Presence Chamber' 175.
Supplement to Historic Doubts 72, 81.

Tamerlane, Epilogue to. See Epilogue.
Tavistock, Francis Russell (1739–67), styled Marquis of 164.
Temple, Anne Chambers (*ca.* 1709–77), Countess, *Poems* 130.
Testament Politique du Chevalier Robert Walpoole 81.
Theodore of Corsica, Account of 43.
Thirlby, Styan (1686?–1753) 32.
'Thoughts on keeping holy the Sabbath, by J. Cardan' 177.
Thoughts on Tragedy and on Comedy 81, 138.
Three Letters to the Whigs 32, 36.
'Three Vernons, The' 164.
'To Britannia' 177.
'To Edward Jerningham' 165.
'To Lady Craven' 84.
'To Love' 84.
'To the Authoress of some lines on Strawberry Hill' 163.

[187]

INDEX

'Toby,' HW's *pseud.* 162.
Tonson, J. and R., publishers 129, 171.
Toynbee, Paget, editor 93, 98, 152, 166.
Toynbee, Mrs. Paget, editor 93.
Turner, R. S., editor 98, 99.

Upper Ossory, Countess of. *See* Liddell, Anne.

Valpy, Richard (1754–1836) 147.
Van Der Dort (Doort), Abraham (d. 1640), editor 120.
Vernon, Joseph (1738?–82) 159.
Verses at Middleton Stoney 172.
'Verses in Memory of King Henry the Sixth' 42.
Verses in Memory of the Marquis of Tavistock 164.
Verses for the Monument of Queen Catherine 164.
'Verses occasioned by a late Will' 155.
Verses on Celia 83.
Verses on the Fireworks for the Peace 176.
Verses to General Conway 159.
Verses to John Dodd 175.
Verses to Lady Temple 130.
Verses to Mrs. Pitt 166.
'Verses to my Pen' 166.
Verses to Zelinda 175.
Vertue, George (1684–1756), engraver and editor 28, 120, 121, 122.
Villiers, George (1628–87), 2d D. of Buckingham 122, 124.
Vindication of the Conduct of the present War 171.
Vision, The 21.
Voltaire (François-Marie Arouet) (1694–1778) 54, 55, 71.

Waldegrave, Geoffrey Noel, 12th Earl Waldegrave, his collection of Walpolian books and MSS 14, and *passim.*
Waller Collection 14, 19, 43, 62, 73, 79, 83, 98, 152, 154, 157, 167.
Walpole, Horace, Books edited by 10;
　Letters of Edward the Sixth 136.
　Life of Lord Herbert of Cherbury 130.
　Mémoires du Comte de Grammont 136.
　Miscellaneous Antiquities 136.
Walpole, Horace, Books published by:
　Hentzner's *Journey* 125.
　Lady Temple's *Poems* 130.
　Letters of Edward the Sixth 136.
　Life of Lord Herbert of Cherbury 130.
　Mémoires du Comte de Grammont 136.
　Miscellaneous Antiquities 136.
　Whitworth's *Account of Russia* 128.
Walpole, Horace, Books with notes or additions by:
　Cambridge *Gratulatio* 105.
　Gough's *Sepulchral Monuments* 143.
　Granger's *Biographical History* 130.
　Hawkins's *History of Music* 175.
　Lysons's *Environs of London* 175.
　Mason's *Poems* 152.
　Notes on Lord Chesterfield's Works 98.
　Notes on Several Characters of Shakespeare 101.
　'Notes on the Exhibitions of the Society of Artists and the Free Society' 167.
　Notes on the Poems of Pope 98.
　Ranby's *Narrative* 107.
　Sir C. H. Williams's *Works* 149.
Walpole, Horace, Books with Prefaces by. *See* Prefaces by HW.
Walpole, Horace, Prologues and Epilogues by. *See* Prologues.
Walpole, Horace. *See further* under individual titles.
Walpole, Horatio (1678–1757), 1st Baron Walpole 171, 172, 173.
Walpole, Horatio (1752–1822), 2d Earl of the 3d creation 172.
Walpole, Sir Robert (1676–1745) 19, 107, 171.
Walpole, Sir Spencer (1839–1907), editor 93.
Walpole, Thomas (1727–1803) 162, 173.
Walpoliana 145–147.
Walpoliana, by Lord Hardwicke 146.
'Walpoliana,' edited by Paget Toynbee from HW's *Books of Materials* and *Paris Journals* 166.
Warburton, Eliot (1810–52), *Memoirs of HW* 149, 151.
Ward, Anne (d. 1789), printer 139.
Watts, Elizabeth, bookseller in Dublin 54.
Webb, W., printer 20, 34, 36, 39.

[188]

INDEX

Wedderburn, Alexander (1733–1805), his Character by HW 177.
Wentworth Castle, HW's verses on 178.
Wentworth, William (1722–91), 2d E. of Strafford 178.
West, Richard (1716–42), HW's letters to 93.
Whaley, John, *Collection of original Poems and Translations* 170; *Journey to Houghton* 26; *The Miser* 170.
'What a rout do you make' 84.
White, Benjamin (d. 1794), publisher 73.
Whiteliver, Richard 39.
Whitworth, Charles (1675–1725), Lord Whitworth, *Account of Russia* 48, 128.
Whytt, Robert, *Essay on the Virtues of Lime-water* 171.
Wilkes, John (1727–97) 47.
Willes, Sir John (1685–1761), Chief Justice 34.
Williams, Sir Charles Hanbury (1708–59) 20, 109; *Works* 149.
Williams, John, publisher 50.
Williams, Robert Folkestone, editor 149.
Williams, T. E., editor 147.
Woburn Abbey 85, 87.
Wolcot, John (Peter Pindar), Verses addressed to HW 170.
Works, The, ed. by Mary Berry 75–85; SH edition 75, 78.
World, The 43, 157, 158, 170.
'World Extraordinary' 157.
Wright, John (1770?–1844), editor 91, 155.
Wyatt, Thomas, HW's life of 136.

Xo Ho, HW's Letter from 39–42, 48.

Yates, Mrs. Mary Ann (1728–87) 138.
Yorke, Philip (1720–90), 2d E. of Hardwicke 147.
Yvon, Paul 149.